Reparation for Slavery and Colonialism:
The Teachings of Durban

Lang Fafa Dampha

Reparation for Slavery and Colonialism:
The Teachings of Durban

By the same author

i. Nationalism and Reparation in West Africa, L'Harmattan, April 2013.

ii. *Afrique subsaharienne : mémoire, histoire et réparation.* L'Harmattan June 2013.

iii. The United Nations, the Bretton Woods Institutions and African Reconstruction, L'Harmattan, September 2014.

iv. Alien Attitude (novel), CreateSpace, June, 2015

v. African Migrants (novel), CreateSpace, August, 2015

In honour of my late beloved uncle and friend,
Alhadji Kebba Fatou Dampha,
Rest in perfect peace.

The wealth of the imperial countries is our wealth too... For in a very concrete way Europe is puffed up inordinately with the gold and raw materials of the colonial countries: Latin America, China, Africa. From all these continents, in front of which Europe today displays its opulent tower, diamonds and oil, silk and cotton, wood and exotic products have been taken for centuries to that same Europe. Europe is literally the creation of the Third World.[1]

Frantz Fanon - The Wretched of the Earth (*Les Damnés de la Terre*).

---

[1] *La richesse des pays impériaux est aussi notre richesse... Très concrètement l'Europe s'est enflée de façon démesurée de l'or et des matières premières des pays coloniaux : Amérique latine, Chine, Afrique. De tous ces continents, en face desquels l'Europe aujourd'hui dresse sa tour opulente, partent depuis des siècles, en direction de cette même Europe les diamants et le pétrole, la soie et le coton, les bois et produits exotiques. L'Europe est littéralement la création du tiers-monde.*

Table of Contents

Introduction

The adoption of the Universal Declaration of Human Rights in 1948 led to the enactment of a number of laws and the adoption of numerous human rights instruments, including the International Convention on the Elimination of All Forms of Racial Discrimination (ICERD) of the United Nations (UN). These were made possible by the commitment of the member states of the UN to eradicate racial discrimination, consequently leading to enormous progress in combating racism and related intolerance.

A series of conferences were subsequently organised by the United Nations and its specialised institutions in 1978, 1983, 2001 and 2009, all in Geneva, Switzerland, except the third World Conference against Racism, Racial Discrimination, Xenophobia and Related Intolerance, which took place in the South African city of Durban, from August 31 to September 08, 2001.

The victory of the African National Congress (ANC), the African Union (AU) and the rest of the international community over apartheid were amongst the factors that influenced the organisation of the third World Conference against Racism. Other contributory factors were the advocacy of numerous non-governmental organisations, and their fight against racism around the globe, a well-organised reparations lobby in the international community, and the commitment by Mary Robinson, the then United Nations High Commissioner for Human Rights, to make the conference the centerpiece of her tenure and a landmark in the struggle against racism. Thus in resolution 52/111, the General Assembly of the United Nations in 1997 decided, also against the background of rising incidents of racism, to hold this third World Conference against Racism, Racial Discrimination, Xenophobia and Related Intolerance, in Durban, South Africa by 2001. As we have noted, South Africa's experience in defeating the institutionalised racism of apartheid and putting in place the process of truth and reconciliation for a peaceful transition to democracy motivated the choice of Durban for the third World Conference against Racism known as Durban I. It was an attempt to develop a new world vision to combat and eradicate racism, designed to be the foremost global human rights conference in the new millennium.

The objectives of the conference were to identify the sources, causes, victims, forms and contemporary manifestations of racism; to develop and provide methods of prevention, effective remedies, compensatory measures and strategies for achieving effective cooperation and enhancement of the United Nations, and other mechanisms for effective combat against racism.

The April 2009 World Conference against Racism which followed Durban I, was held in Geneva. It was formally known as the Durban Review Conference, and aimed at assessing the programmes and fast-tracking the implementation of the measures and action plan adopted at the 2001 Durban I World Conference against Racism.

The Durban World Conference against Racism was viewed by many as the genuine and appropriate setting to pursue reparation especially for slavery, and the moment at which the details of reparation could be negotiated, with the hope that the Draft Declaration and Programme of Action would furnish guidelines for reparation. Therefore, the African Union, non-governmental organisations and civil society groups around the world, including a significant number from the United States, lobbied widely during the series of preparatory regional meetings to ensure that the conference agenda reflected their demands.

Sub-Saharan Africa and its Diaspora therefore took the issue of reparation for slavery, colonialism and apartheid[2]

---

[2] We will intermittently refer to apartheid as one of the "crimes against humanity" for which reparation has been claimed, even though the Republic of South Africa has undertaken its own process of reconciliation and reparation.

whose consequences have been well documented and debated for a very long time, as the theme of the 2001 Durban Conference against Racism, to define their positions and claim compensation as reparation for the effects of these phenomena on the people of African descent.

Reparation claim for slavery is not a new phenomenon, because the African Diaspora and other social groups in the Americas have a long history of demanding compensation for the wrongs inflicted on them, particularly in terms of slavery. For example, in the United States, the Black Panthers in the 1960s recalled the promise of "Forty Acres and a Mule."[3]

West Germany made a massive reparation payment to the State of Israel and to individual Jewish families for the collective crime of Germany against Jews during the Hitler era. "Between 1953 and 1992, the Federal Republic of (West) Germany paid out more than $35 billion in reparation to the Zionist state and to millions of individual victims of the Holocaust" (ihr.org).

To redress the historic injustice of the United States to Japanese-Americans, the US Senate in 1988 apologised, and voted overwhelmingly in favour of awarding $20,000 each to the Japanese-Americans who were driven from their homes and sent to internment camps by the Roosevelt Administration during World War II. (The New York

---

[3] Forty Acres and a Mule described a promise freed slaves believed the U.S. government had made at the end of the Civil War. Many freedmen believed they had a moral right to own the land they had long worked as slaves, and were eager to control their own property. A rumour, which had its origin in an order issued by General William Tecumseh Sherman of the U.S. Army in January 1865, spread throughout the South that land belonging to plantation owners would be given to former slaves so that they could set up their own farms. Following the capture of Savannah, Georgia, General Sherman, ordered that abandoned plantations along the Georgia and South Carolina coasts be divided up and plots of land be given to freed blacks. However, the order never became a permanent government policy. Consequently, lands confiscated from former Confederates were later returned to them by the administration of President Andrew Johnson and the freed slaves were evicted from their 40 acres (16 ha) farmland.

Times, April 21, 1988.) The US government in 2012 also approved payment of $1billion compensation to the 41 Indian tribes over century-old claims for spoliation of their lands (dailymail.co.uk).

Some commentators and activists in Africa and the African Diaspora tried to justify the pertinence of reparation for slavery and/or colonisation. The Martinican psychiatrist and writer, Frantz Fanon, in his book, *The Wretched of the Earth*, argued in favour of reparation, that the wealth of Europe was attributable to the colonial exploitation of Africa, through colonial projects. For Fanon then the countries that benefited from the colonial operation should pay compensation to newly independent countries; he further argued that material or financial reparation should be appropriate to post-colonial Africa if they contribute to the restoration of justice.

Back in the 19th century, some African-American Congressmen introduced bills to seek reparation on behalf of former slaves, but without success. The issue of reparation for slavery in the United States then fell into oblivion. In 1964, both Min. Malcolm X (later El-Hajj Malik El-Shabazz) as the national spokesperson for the Nation of Islam[4] and Rev. Martin Luther King Jr., head of the Civil Rights Movement, took up the issue. In his book, *Why We Cannot Wait*, King argued that the exploitation and humiliation that black people have suffered cannot be quantified; even the wealth of the United States cannot compensate it (King 25).

A Michigan (African-American) Congressman, John Conyers, took up the issue in 1989 and introduced bill H.R. 40, to study reparation proposals for descendants of slaves in the United States. The title of his bill, HR 40, symbolised

---

[4]A movement that advocated the establishment of an independent nation of people of African descent in or outside the United States, and that the federal government should pay reparation to African Americans, as compensation for unpaid slave labour over the centuries.

the United States' Forty Acres and a Mule "unfulfilled promise" to freed slaves, and the devastation of slavery on the lives of African-Americans, which the United States Government has never officially recognised. Conyers' bill did not aim at direct reparation; it merely sought to recognise the inhumanity and injustice of slavery, and create a committee to examine its consequence in terms of discrimination. The committee was also to make recommendations to Congress on suitable measures that would redress the effect on African-Americans. (conyers.house.gov) He argued that the United States became what it is today, "the most prosperous country in the free world," thanks to the work of African slaves, and that the people who through coercion contributed to this national prosperity have never been paid, but harassed and humiliated; therefore their descendants should be reimbursed for that which their grandparents never received (ibid). Conyers' bill, however, failed; he introduced it each year as he had promised, but in vain. Politically, the idea of compensating victims of slavery led to no tangible result in the United States. Nevertheless, it did not cease to grow in importance among the African-American community, especially since the decision by Congress in 1988 to apologise and pay reparations to Japanese-Americans interned in camps during World War II. Several other black personalities in the United States, including Rev. Jesse Louis Jackson, Sr., founder and president of the Rainbow PUSH Coalition,[5] and one of the United States prominent civil, religious and political rights personalities, took up the issue again in the 20th century in their writings and conferences. Court cases were also filed in 2002, in New York and New Jersey against the U.S. government and companies involved in the slave trade, such as Fleet Boston Financial, Aetna and CSX[6] (usatoday30.usatoday.com).

---

[5] A social justice organisation devoted to African-Americans' political empowerment, education and changing public policy.

The Faculty Fellow Emeritus at the Berkman Center, and Co-Chair of the Reparations Coordinating Committee,[7] Professor Charles Ogletree of Harvard University, supported these actions. Randall N. Robinson, founder and president of TransAfrica,[8] is another African-American personality who defended the thesis of reparation for slavery in the United States. In his book, *The Debt: What America Owes to Blacks*, Robinson argued that just as Germany and other parties involved in the Holocaust owed reparation to Jews, the United States and other parties that played a role in and benefitted:

> ...from the slave trade owed reparations to the blacks following the holocaust of African slavery which has carried forward from slavery's inception for 350-odd years to the end of U.S. government-embraced racial discrimination—an end that arrived, it would seem, only just yesterday. (18)

Descendants of African slaves sued Lloyds Bank in London in 2004, for its role in the Trans-Atlantic slave trade, unsuccessfully; and in the same year, a coalition of Rastafari movement groups in Jamaica claimed 72.5 billion pound Sterling from the British government as compensation for slavery, to relocate 500,000 Jamaican Rastafarians in Africa. Britain rejected the claim on the grounds that it could not be accountable for wrongs in the past centuries. In 2007, the

---

[6]Fleet Boston was born from a bank established by a merchant whose ships transported African slaves. Aetna is an insurance company that insured the human property of slave owners, not to protect their slaves, but as a protection of their investment in the event of the slaves' deaths. Chessie System Xpress (CSX) grew from a company that used slave labor to build railways.

[7] A group of lawyers and other experts researching a lawsuit based upon a claim of reparations for descendants of African slaves.

[8]TransAfrica (formerly TransAfrica Forum) was founded in 1977 by Randall Robinson as an African-American lobby to seek to influence the foreign policy of the United States on Africa and the Caribbean countries and all African diaspora groups. Randall Robinson remained as President of the organisation until 2001.

Guyanese President, Bharrat Jagdeo while addressing a commemorative ceremony for the bicentenary of the abolition of the Trans-Atlantic slave trade "called for European nations to pay reparations for the horrors of the slave trade" (bbc.co.uk).

The leader of the Nation of Islam, Honourable Min. Louis Abdul Farrakhan, has also contributed to the quest for reparation for slavery in the United States. At a conference on reparation held in the United States, in January 2010, he alluded to the reparation of billions of dollars made to Japanese-Americans and the Indian tribes by the United States government. Also making special reference to the reparation made to the Jewish State and to individual Jewish families by the German government for the Holocaust that affected approximately six million Jews, he argued:

> According to the late, great scholar W.E.B. Du Bois, a conservative estimate of Black lives lost in the Middle Passage was from 50 to 100 million Black lives. We don't need to minimize the Jewish Holocaust. Six million lives is a lot of lives, but are you telling me that six million white lives are more valuable than 100 million Black lives? [...] Three hundred years working from "can't see morning to can't see night," for no pay. Three hundred years working millions of slaves for nothing. [...] The killing of our fathers and mothers after mating them like animals, then taking the children and naming us after the slave master, stripping us of our language, our God, our religion, our minds. [...] The destruction of our families. (finalcall.com)

The Caribbean island State of Antigua and Barbuda, through the voice of its Prime Minister and Minister for Foreign Affairs, Winston Baldwin Spencer, on 24 September 2011, demanded reparation for injustices suffered by African slaves and their descendants, arguing at the United Nations that violence and segregation against people of African descent had compromised their capability for progress. He emphasised that former slave-trading States should formally apologise for the crimes they committed over the 400 years of the African slave trade, arguing that:

> None should disagree that racism and other legacies of slavery continue to shape the lives of people of African descent – thus reparations must be directed toward repairing the damage inflicted by slavery and racism [...] And to help counter the lingering damage inflicted on generations of peoples of African descent by generations of slave-trading and colonialism, we call on those very States to back up their apologies with new commitments to the economic development of the nations that have suffered from this human tragedy. (un.org)

Jamaica renewed its reparations claim in 2012, by creating a commission to consider the question of whether the country should seek an apology or reparation from Britain for its role in the slave trade. However the opposition argued that taking into account Britain's role in the ending of the slave trade, it should not pay reparations for its role in the slave trade (jamaicaobserver.com).

The government of Barbados, in the same year established a 12-member Reparations Task Force, chaired by Professor Pedro Welch, which would take care of maintaining the momentum for reparation, and it is calling for reparation from former slave-owning and colonial powers for the injustices suffered by the people of African descent and their families. According to Culture Minister Stephen Lashley, the Task force will "...further the research and publication of works that make the case for reparations and self-reparations at individual, community, national, regional and international levels, among other things" (atlantablackstar.com). The project was geared to include government collaborating with the University of the West Indies to organise a regional reparation conference to form a Caribbean commission and establish a Multi-ethnic Research

Centre, a National Museum on Slavery and a Centre for Reparations Research.

In 2013, during the commemoration of the 250th anniversary of the Berbice Slave Revolt, in British Guyana in 1763, marked by a series of lectures in Georgetown, Guyana, for an "informed and sensible conversation" on what was considered "the worst crime against humanity," slavery, the noted historian, Sir Hilary Beckles, Principal of the Cape Hill Campus of the University of West Indies, "urged Caribbean countries to emulate the position adopted by the Jews who were persecuted during the Second World War and have since organised the Jewish Reparation Fund" (jamaicaobserver.com).

The claims for reparation by African-Americans addressed to the United States government did not, however, visibly invoke reparation on behalf of Africans on the continent either for slavery or colonialism, which obliges us to consider the issue of reparation proper to the African continent. The position of the early advocates, especially in the United States neglecting reparation concerning colonialism is attributed to the fact that the bulk of their demand dated to a time when some parts of Africa were still under colonial rule.

In Sub-Saharan Africa the issue of compensation as a fundamental claim for reparation of the effects of the slave trade, colonisation and apartheid on the people of Africa dates to the post-independence era. It was Anglophone West Africa which, as in the case of the struggle for African decolonisation, took the first steps to claim reparation. In 1992, Chief Moshood Kashimawo Olawale Abiola of Nigeria proposed the creation of a Group of Eminent Personalities within the Organisation of African Unity (OAU) to study the issue of reparation. Consequently the summit of Heads of State and Government of the Member States of the OAU, held in Dakar, Senegal, from 29 June to 01 July 1992, appointed a committee of personalities to study the question of reparation to victims in Africa and the African Diaspora. Subsequently, in 1993 the first Pan-African Congress addressing the issue of reparation was held in Abuja, Nigeria, with delegates from about thirty countries; Dr. Salim Ahmed Salim, Secretary General of the OAU 1989-2001, was amongst the participants. At the end of the meeting, delegates adopted the Abuja Proclamation affirming their commitment to obtaining reparation for slavery and colonialism. The Congress also called for national reparation committees to be established throughout Africa and the African Diaspora, which led to the creation of the African Reparation Movement (ARM)[9].

In 1999, the Ghanaian capital, Accra, welcomed representatives of African governments for a conference on the issue of reparation, under the name of the African World Reparations and Repatriation Truth Commission (AWRRTC). The Accra Declaration claimed $777 trillion as compensation from all the nations of Western Europe and the Americas, as well as from institutions that participated and benefited from the slave trade and colonialism. The Accra Declaration also demanded that the external debt of Africa be cancelled as part of the compensation, because the deterioration of the socio-economic condition of the African continent has directly been related to Africa's debt crisis, which was primarily engendered by the phenomena in question.

Is the OAU/AU claim for reparation on behalf of Africa tangible? It is necessary to analyse the claims for reparation, especially those made at the Durban Conference against Racism in 2001 and the subsequent World Conference against Racism, organised in 2009 in Geneva, and the terms

---

[9]An organisation in Britain chaired by high-profile Labour Member of Parliament, Bernie Grant (1944-2000), established after the 1993 Conference on Reparations in Abuja, Nigeria. ARM sought reparation for the enslavement and colonisation of the African people. After the death of its Chairperson, the movement is not active; a campaign for African reparation is however taking place on its Facebook page.

involved, taking into account the position of the African Diaspora, especially in the United States, concerning the claim for reparation for slavery. We have also to try to reconcile the contradictory positions, to possibly eventually identify ways and means of the process. What is the meaning of reparation in Sub-Saharan Africa's process of reconstruction and development?

Reparation dates back to the *lex talionis,* which in Latin means "the law of retaliation" in early Babylonian law, present in both biblical and early Roman law. According to its principles:

> ...criminals should receive as punishment precisely those injuries and damages they had inflicted upon their victims. Many early societies applied this "eye-for-an-eye" principle literally... Talion was the ultimate satisfaction a plaintiff might demand but was not mandatory; the injured person could obtain satisfaction with money if he wished. ("Talion")

Reparation according to this early Babylonian model therefore represented punishment that corresponded to the injuries inflicted on victims, and which could, as we have just seen, be claimed in monetary terms.

For the National Coalition of Blacks for Reparations in America (N'COBRA)[10], reparation is:

> ...a process of repairing, healing and restoring a people injured because of their group identity and in violation of their fundamental human rights by governments or corporations. [...] In addition to being a demand for justice, it is a principle of international human rights law. As a remedy, it is similar to the remedy for damages in domestic law that holds a person responsible for injuries suffered by another when the infliction of the injury violates domestic law. (katrinareader.org)

Unlike the Babylonian model, which was based more on the notion of punishment and/or revenge corresponding to the damage caused by the perpetrator, this N'COBRA vision goes further to evoke the healing of injuries and restoring

---

[10]An American coalition established in 1987 with the sole objective of seeking financial compensation for the descendants of former slaves in the United States. N'COBRA's organisational founders are the National Conference of Black Lawyers, the New Afrikan Peoples Organisation, and the Republic of New Afrika. It has individual members and organisational affiliates.

their effects. It therefore also entails the disbursement of compensation for an offence or crime, to redress its effects, commonly in material form.

African leaders have claimed compensation from the West for the damages done to the continent by the institutions of the slave trade, and colonisation. This would supposedly help Africa to regain its dignity and stand on its own two feet to equitably and effectively compete in international trade and politics. However, from an additional and important angle, the notion of reparation in this work puts emphasis also on the dutiful participation of Africans themselves as well in a nationalistic perspective. Reparation, reconstruction and development[11] are therefore linked in the context of African history and post-colonialism. As an instrument of African reparation, we are therefore considering the comprehensive notion of development, including all the aspects of life: the economy, the society and culture, as well as the environment that has been affected and needs to be redressed.

For reparation as a form of development to be sustainable, its principles must appropriately come from within the society and must also be effectively managed by the people concerned. It must meet the purpose of the exercise without compromising the development needs of the future generations. The concept of reparation we are dealing with is therefore appropriate and maintainable reconstruction as part of a whole development process, which would serve as a bridge between Africa and the outside world, notably the West, and even the Arab world as far as the history of slavery and colonialism is concerned. The practical concept of African reparation in this work therefore refers to appropriate, effective and sustainable efforts, first by Africans themselves, to heal the grave wounds caused by the three historical phenomena that

---

[11]Reconstruction, reparation and development are interchangeably used in this work.

dominated and affected African history; it is therefore a process of development initiated, engineered, promoted and controlled by Africans themselves as an appropriate and progressive form of reconstruction and/or reparation.

The slave trade, colonialism and apartheid have been considered by most observers as factors of socio-economic destructiveness of the African continent. Numerous commentators have argued that slavery removed at least ten million able-bodied men and women from Africa within a period of five centuries. Honourable Louis Farakhan, evoking W.E.B. Du Bois, advanced an estimate of 100 million lost black lives.

Chief Moshood Abiola formally defending the view that a wrong committed should be repaired, claimed that Africa should be compensated in the form of massive investment in the education, agriculture and health sectors. Abiola's demand for reparation was visibly not confined to direct financial compensation.

We have seen that the African Diaspora in the United States did not include colonialism in their claim for compensation, assuming that it was because parts of Africa were then still under colonial domination. The group of eminent persons of the Organisation of African Unity for their part examined the two phenomena: slavery and colonialism, through which, according to them, the West exploited the continent to promote its own development. We can see that the OAU committee of personalities, in their turn, did not include apartheid, simply because, just like the case of the compensation claims by African-Americans not considering the issue of colonisation, apartheid was not yet over; when the O.A.U. meeting took place.

The issue of reparations for the African continent and its Diaspora is therefore not new; it was developed in the 19th century and concerns the memory of mankind, or at least that of the victims. We will see how to reconcile the claim for financial compensation of African-Americans on the

23

question of slavery on the one hand, and that of Africans on the continent in a general context, on the other. To define the morale that African observers attach to reparation, it is necessary to consider the arguments, especially those presented during the third World Conference against Racism in Durban, in 2001.

We have said that reparation means correcting injustices of the past and the present conditions caused by the wrong acts, so that victims can be rehabilitated. Our original definition did not clarify the ways and means in which it should be carried out, but the claim originating from Africans and African-Americans spoke clearly about it. Many African-American commentators including Rev. Martin Luther King Jr., Randall Robinson and Professor Charles Ogletree all evoked financial reparation from the American government for having enslaved black people on a massive scale. However, we have suggested that the concept of reparation is much broader than the financial component most observers attached to it. Both Frantz Fanon and Chief Moshood Abiola viewed reparation in the context of the historical experience and the contemporary situation generated by this experience, hence beyond the simple material aspect of it, although this material component in some ways also aims at some form of rehabilitation and the establishment of social justice.

The African continent has been considered the first civilisation on this planet, but it is now perceptibly the most remote and backward especially in terms of socio-economic development. It has been considered as one of the richest continents in terms of natural resources, yet it is today the poorest on the globe in terms of material wealth. According to some observers, this is due to the reduction of the continent by several centuries of exploitation, whose legacy is perpetual, in this era of globalisation. Thus, the basic idea of African reparation is to remedy this exploitation and marginalisation so that Sub-Saharan Africa and its Diaspora are fully liberated and equipped to participate in globalisation in normal terms.

In all cases reparation involves the parties who were once in conflict, namely the perpetrators, who become the potential payers on the one hand and the victims who are the potential beneficiaries on the other. It is not, as we have noticed, simply confined to material compensation, but also incorporates a moral aspect. The material aspect refers to compensation in monetary terms, and the moral side covers all that concerns repentance, remorse, apology…, with a genuine willingness to dialogue so as to redress the negative conditions that were engendered by those wrongs. Reconciliation is therefore somehow also a precondition for most forms of reparation, at least superficially since the sides that were once antagonists should come to terms in the absence of retributive justice, even if it might be hard to overlook the conflict that engineered the reconciliation process in question. Both the monetary and moral aspects should engage contributors and recipients, leading to reconciliation and cooperation. In this perspective, if the West and the Arab world have a duty towards contributing to redressing the socio-economic problems of the African continent for having perpetrated the three phenomena that devastated the continent, especially Sub-Saharan Africa, the African peoples have even a greater duty towards the process of redressing the ills of their own continent, hence African reparation requires Africans to act primarily.

What then should exactly be the role of Africans in this reparation process? What are the positions of the former slave-trading and colonising countries vis-à-vis the issue of reparation? What can they contribute to Sub-Saharan Africa's reconstruction, while the relationships have changed? What is the rationale and relevance of Africa's claim for reparation?

The Blair Commission: factor of African reparation?

Africa has been independent for more than 60 years, but it is still adversely affected by precariousness and marginalisation in international relations, and hence has not been able to independently and effectively carry out its own development programmes.

Governments, inter-governmental and non-governmental organisations and even individuals, both in and outside Africa, especially those who might be considered as having moral obligations towards helping the continent to surmount its problems, have therefore made attempts to initiate ways of alleviating Africa's socio-economic problems as a contribution to its reparation programme. For example, in Kananaskis, Canada, in 2002, the G8[12] adopted an action plan for Africa. In early 2004, the British government, through the initiative of its Prime Minister, Tony Blair, established a Commission for Africa to study and propose strategies to provide stimulus for Africa's development. Consequently at the Gleneagles summit in Scotland in July 2005, the G8 expressed their commitment to reducing poverty in Africa. Musicians Bono and Bob Geldof also organised huge concerts in the same year to raise international awareness about the situation in Africa. In 2006, the European Commission, some of whose Member States had been at the centre of the factors of Africa's dispossession, proposed a programme called "Strategy for Africa," which outlined a plan of action for European Union

---

[12]The G8, (Group of Eight), is an assembly (forum) of world leaders from governments of eight leading industrialised countries who meet annually to discuss global issues. It was originally formed by six leading industrialised countries and subsequently extended with two additional members. Russia was invited as the last member to join the group, but has recently been excluded from the group on 24 March, 2014 because of Putin's involvement in the crisis in (Crimea) Ukraine. Each year, the G8 holds a Leaders' Summit, in which Heads of State and Government of member countries meet to discuss and attempt to reconcile global issues.

Member States intending to support Africa's efforts to realise the Millennium Development Goals (MDGs). It is essential to study the Blair Commission for Africa and its potential impact on African reparation, as seemingly the most elaborate amongst all the initiatives and support offered from the outside to help alleviate Africa's socioeconomic problems.

The objective of the Blair Commission for Africa was to generate new ideas for development and to campaign for the implementation of existing international commitments towards development in Africa. The Commission had 17 Commissioners, including 9 Sub-Saharan Africans amongst who were Benjamin Mkapa, President of Tanzania from 1995 to 2005; Mrs Linah Kelebogile Mohohlo, governor of the Bank of Botswana; Meles Zenawi, Prime Minister of Ethiopia from 1995 until his death in 2012; and Tidjane Thiam, Chief Executive Officer of the Prudential, former head of the National Bureau for Technical Studies and Development and later Minister of Planning and Development in Côte d'Ivoire 1994–1999.[13] Tony Blair, British Prime Minister from 1997 to 2007 (initiator and Chairperson of the Commission); Gordon Brown, UK Chancellor of the Exchequer, (later Prime Minister 2007-2010); Hilary Benn,[14] UK Development Minister; Michel

---

[13]The remaining African members of the Commissions are: William Kalema, Managing Director at DCDM Advisory Services Uganda Limited; Anna Tibaijuka, Executive Director of UN-HABITAT; Fola Adeola, founder and chairman of FATE Foundation, a charitable foundation to promote entrepreneurship among the youth in Nigeria; K.Y. Amoako, founder and president of the African Centre for Economic Transformation, an institute that provides governments in Africa with policy research and advice. He was Executive Secretary of the UN Economic Commission for Africa from 1995-2005.

[14]Hilary James Wedgwood Benn was Secretary of State for International Development from 2003 to 2007 and then as the Secretary of State for Environment, Food and Rural Affairs from 2007 to 2010. He is currently, the Shadow Secretary of State for Communities and Local Government.

Camdessus, France's former head of the International Monetary Fund (1987-2000) and Nancy Landon Kassebaum Baker, veteran US Senator, Kansas (1978–1997), were also members of the Commission for Africa. The Blair Commission published its first report entitled "Our Common Interest," on March 11, 2005. Putting forward a coherent package of measures and recommendations to achieve its objectives, it logically recognised that the entire world has a role in and would benefit from, creating a solid and flourishing Africa (commissionforafrica.info).

According to the recommendations of "Our Common Interest" report, the international community should collaborate with Africa to promote governance, increase accountability and transparency, reinforce the information system and combat corruption. Strengthening the domains of peace and security by concentrating on tackling the causes of conflict, and promoting regional and global capacity-building to prevent, resolve and manage conflicts on the continent, and investing in people, especially in the domains of education and health, were also recommended. In the domain of trade and commerce, the report recommended improving Africa's capacity to trade by facilitating its access to the markets of richer countries. Central to the recommendations of the report is the doubling of aid to Sub-Saharan Africa to be increased by US$25 billion annually over the next 5 years. The Commission also recommended debt relief in the perspective of 100 per cent debt cancellation as a component of a financing package for the poor countries in Sub-Saharan Africa to achieve the Millennium Development Goals (MDGs).

Another important aspect of the recommendations was to give Africans greater responsibility and influence in the decision-making in their programmes because they are directly affected; this would also be a way of giving them responsibility for their own development. The report went on to campaign for the strengthening of African multilateral institutions, in that shareholders of major institutions such as the African Development Bank should work towards making the bank the outstanding financing institution of development programmes in Africa. It also called for a campaign for the enhancement of the role of the Economic Commission for Africa and for the management of multilateral organisations such as the World Bank (WB), the International Monetary Fund (IMF), and the World Trade Organisation (WTO) to change their strategies and give more priorities to development in Africa.

The majority of the recommendations of the Commission were considered by the G8 leaders during their meeting that subsequently took place at Gleneagles in July 2005, and by other major international gatherings with commitments made that year. Concerning funding the programmes of the Commission for Africa, donor countries and international financial institutions would commit funds through an International Finance Facility (IFF). Further mechanisms in the form of international levies to raise additional finance, such as charges on airline tickets were also proposed.

Part of the recommendations of the Commission was to give African countries a greater voice in multilateral institutions like the World Bank, the IMF and the WTO, by according them greater representation on their Boards of Governors or Administrators, hence in the strategic leadership and decision-making in these institutions. This is in line with the 2005 report of the Commission that the strategic leadership and decision-making in these multilateral institutions should be the responsibility of the political leaders of their Member States. The Commission for Africa thus recommended the establishment of "a decision-making Council" of political representatives of Member States, for these institutions. Equally important was the idea that the criteria for appointing the heads of these international organisations and institutions should be based on competition, instead of the traditional appointments according to nationality. Also the United Nation should enlarge its Security Council and other organs to include greater African representation.

Following the massive global campaign of the Blair Commission for Africa, the G8 at their July 2005 Gleneagles summit promised to implement at least half of the Commission's recommendations; other major international commitments were made as well. These included doubling previous levels of aid for basic education; $36bn of debt relief by 100% debt cancellation; the launch of the UN Central Emergency Response Fund (CERF);[15] cancellation of school fees; scaling up of efforts to boost girls' education and female literacy; working more closely with the African Union and the New Partnership for Africa's Development (NEPAD), which is now an integral part of the African Union; putting in place mechanisms to return cash looted by dictators and kept in Western banks to their legitimate owners, and making African governments more accountable to their people (ibid).

Five years after the publication of its first report, the Commission for Africa published a second report in 2010, entitled "Still our Common Interests" which, as a follow-up, evaluated the situation in Africa since 2005. It conducted an audit of progress against each of the recommendations made in the previous report and made further recommendations for the next steps to be taken. (ibid) The new report celebrated the progress made by Africa in the past five years, and called on African governments to continue their efforts to promote growth and to channel revenues into key services and poverty reduction programmes. African leaders

---

[15]The Central Emergency Response Fund (CERF) was established by the General Assembly of the United Nations in December 2005 and launched in March 2006 as a humanitarian fund to enable early action and response for more timely and reliable humanitarian assistance to those affected by natural disasters and armed conflicts as a means of reducing loss of life.

must also make sure that economic growth led to the reduction of poverty for ordinary citizens and for the promotion of development on the continent. The 2010 report equally called for donors and the international community to increase their support for Africa and its capacity-building efforts. It made more recommendations on measures to be taken both by African governments and the developed countries, so as to accelerate development on the continent.

African governments should:

i. Continue their efforts to make it easier to do business between and within their countries – including investing in much needed infrastructure and ensuring that they are collecting the revenues from growth through improved domestic resource mobilisation;
ii. Meet their commitments to spending on health, education, water and sanitation, and agriculture;
iii. Develop and deliver clear strategies to create jobs, reduce poverty and strengthen key services such as health and education.

Developed countries were also urged to:

i. Support African governments' own strategies for promoting growth and development;
ii. Help Africa negotiate the best deals possible for the exploitation of its natural resources by supporting a fund to pay for the legal and technical advice to do this;
iii. Kick-start long-delayed reform of international trade rules;
iv. Continue to support Africa's development – including supporting a Global Fund for Education and providing additional financing to adapt to climate change;
v. Agree that the G20 take on the G8's previous role in making and monitoring commitments to supporting growth and development in Africa (ibid).

According to the two reports combined, development in Africa required a series of steps; and African governments should be allowed to take the responsibility for and control their own process, with the support of the international community. However, none of the two reports recommended concrete ways of solving Africa's massive debt problem that obviously has been harmful to its process of development. The 2005 report urged the developed countries to cancel the debt of Sub-Saharan African countries, which led to the G8's decision to cancel 100 percent of the public debt of some Third World countries, including some African countries, within the framework of the Initiative for Heavily Indebted Poor Countries (HIPC). There were however only 18 African countries on the global list of 62 selected by the Millennium Development Goals (MDGs) of the United Nations. According to the European Network on Debt and Development, (Eurodad) based in Brussels, this decision was insufficient, especially in relation to the objectives set by the United Nations.

Also, the conception of the funds that the Commission would provide Africa with, which as we have seen would be through the implementation of a programme called International Finance Facility (IFF), was not precisely defined. Countries, mainly in the West, and some international financial institutions would commit funds to finance the programme in the form of loans with terms of engagement to be abided by the beneficiaries. Also central to the Commission's scheme are Public Private Partnerships (PPP) according to which the private sector would be contracted to implement development projects like roads and to provide basic services like electricity and water, because of the conventional belief that private companies are more efficient. However, the service provision of the private sector is often more expensive, which usually creates price increase, making these services almost unaffordable by the poor, hence excluding them. This strategy also risked handing control of public companies that produce goods and services of basic necessities such as water and electricity

33

to foreign private companies, which risked compromising their social vocation and developmental role at large.

The reports correctly highlighted that the African continent has been marginalised on the international scene, especially in multilateral organisations like the United Nations (UN), the International Monetary Fund (IMF), the World Bank (WB) and the World Trade Organisation (WTO), but fell short of specifying that one of the major factors of this marginalisation has been in relation to Africa's non-membership of the United Nations Security Council with veto power, which is a prominent aspect of African reparation.

The reports, especially the first one, originally had a major impact on global policy decisions, but this impact diminished after the Gleneagles summit, and only a few of the recommendations which were pledged at Gleneagles, such as the cancellation of the public debt of some countries from the South, including some Sub-Saharan African countries, were implemented. Consequently the Africa Progress Panel (APP), chaired by former United Nations Secretary General Kofi Annan, (including Tony Blair, Michel Camdessus, Tidjane Thiam and Bob Geldof) was launched in April 2007 to campaign and remind world leaders to deliver their promises and commitments to Africa.

The effectiveness of the strategies and measures seemed therefore doubtful, for the simple historic reason that most pledges, especially those made to Africa by Western governments and institutions were not honoured. For example, in Kananaskis, Canada, in 2002, the G8 adopted an action plan for Africa; but it was never honoured. In 2006, the European Commission's proposal of a programme called "Strategy for Africa," was considered more as a response to the massive flow of African immigrants to Spain via Morocco, rather than a genuine commitment to participate in African reparation.

Also donors or lenders of most forms of aid, directly or indirectly regain more than double the aid through loan and interest repayment, and usually impose the purchase of their goods and services on the borrowers, which sometimes equals 90 percent of the fund, according to the British non-governmental organisation, Action Aid (actionaid.org.uk). Apart from the direct monetary benefit, lenders might have indirect economic, political and strategic interests which could hamper the very effort of African reparation.

The reports also tend to cast the responsibility for Africa's socio-economic problems more on the behavior of African policy-makers, hence playing down the role of the slave trade, colonialism and apartheid, as well as the post-colonial relationship between Africa and the West, especially its former colonisers.

However, the central idea of the reports of the Commission, to have funds stolen by undemocratic regimes from the people of Africa and deposited in banks in developed countries returned to their rightful owners, was an interesting and remarkable suggestion. This amounts to more than half the total of the external debt of the continent. If the Blair government or its successors implemented this measure, it would be a positive aspect of the contribution by the United Kingdom to African reparation, and would complement the efforts of Prime Minister Blair vis-à-vis Britain's commitment to contribute to African reparation, in spite of their unwillingness to apologise and pay financial compensation.[16] It would have been remarkable if the Commission for Africa genuinely campaigned for the attribution of the legitimate permanent seat with veto power in the UN Security Council that belonged to Africa to enable the continent to play its rightful role in international relations and politics.

---

[16] See Britain's position at the World Conference against Racism, Racial Discrimination, Xenophobia and Related Intolerance, page 40.

We have indicated that most Africans and the African Diaspora considered slavery, colonialism and apartheid as the main causes of their socio-economic precariousness and marginalisation, and that amongst these, slavery is a common factor. Therefore, at the Durban conference, they demanded that the international community qualified slavery, colonialism and apartheid as "crimes against humanity" and that reparation be made to redress the situation. The countries that benefited from the slave trade and colonisation of the African peoples should, therefore, apologise and pay financial compensation to Africa and the African Diaspora.

We have also said that the 2001 World Conference against Racism and Racial Discrimination held in Durban is the third of a series of world conferences against racism, organised under the auspices of the United Nations, and the first in which a claim for reparation for the slave trade, colonialism and apartheid was formally presented and discussed at international level. Throughout the conference, the debate was based on arguments made by participants with naturally different positions. They expressed two distinct views: the one from the West, particularly the United States and the European Union, and the other from Africa, especially Sub-Saharan Africa and the African Diaspora, notably in the United States. There were arguments presented by the two worlds: the descendants of the victims of slavery, colonisation and apartheid against those of perpetrators of the slave trade, and colonisers. "The First World, developed and rich" against another called, "Third World, developing or under-developed and poor."

The conference opened with a speech by Thabo Mbeki, the then President of the host country, South Africa, in its city of Durban, emblematic of the struggle of black people against apartheid. President Mbeki said that:

...there are many in our common world who suffer indignity and humiliation because they are not white. Their cultures and traditions are despised as savage and primitive and their identities denied. They are not white and are deeply immersed in poverty. [...] Our common humanity dictates that as we rose against apartheid racism, so must we combine to defeat the consequences of slavery, colonialism and racism which, to this day, continue to define the lives of billions of people who are brown and black as lives of hopelessness. Nobody ever chose to be a slave, to be colonised, to be racially oppressed. The impulses of the time caused these crimes to be committed by human beings against others. Surely, the impulse of our own time says to all of us that we must do everything we can to free those who to this day suffer from racism, xenophobia and related intolerance because their forebears were enslaved, colonised and racially oppressed..., this World Conference must convey the message that the peoples of the world are inspired by a new internationalism that says that we are determined to unite in action to repair the gross human damage that was caused in the past. (Report, 151, 154)

This opening speech exposes and denounces the indignity and humiliation of racism and discrimination of black people because their ancestors were enslaved. Raising moral issues, it indicates that poverty is not a natural condition, and the condition of being enslaved, colonised, and oppressed through apartheid is not a choice of anyone. Considering slavery, colonialism and apartheid as the main causes of exploitation, poverty and marginalisation of Africans, it invites the delegates to work together to combat and "repair the gross human damage" of the past. It hopes that the racism that continues to define the lives of billions of people worldwide, including Africans, be finally overthrown.

The main argument is that to enable Africa to occupy its deserved place in the world, the authors of the slave trade and colonisation should contribute to repairing the damages caused by their crimes. We have also seen that the process of reconciliation as an essential step can be possible only

38

through consultation and dialogue. Therefore both the perpetrators and the victims should necessarily be collectively involved in the reconciliation process.

As we have seen also, well before the Durban Conference against Racism, Sub-Saharan Africa had expressed its views on the issue of reparation through the voice of Chief Moshood K. O. Abiola of Nigeria to justify its moral aspects. This and the existence in the Diaspora of movements for reparation, such as the National Coalition of Blacks for Reparations in America (N'COBRA) in the United States, and the African Reparation Movement (ARM) in the United Kingdom, symbolised the importance of the issue of reparation to both the African continent and the African Diaspora, especially in the Americas.

Being in the position of defendant, the West pronounced its "deep regret" to the peoples of African descent, but refused to express solemn apology and agree to make reparation. France, through its "Taubira Act,"[17] adopted in 2001, is the first country to qualify slavery as a crime against humanity. This French legislation was, however, criticised by many, especially African observers, as having "been partially emptied of substance... Particularly with regards to the compensation to States and to descendants of slaves"[18] (pyepimanla.com).

The French chief delegate at the Durban Conference, Charles Josselin, the then deputy Minister for Cooperation in France, declared:

Concerning the issue of apology... We were ready to maintain, for our part, the formula proposed by the Belgian Presidency of the European Union, which was that at the Durban Conference, on behalf of all those who had perpetrated these undignified events, should apologise. The advantage of this formula is to include, I would say, all those who share these

---

[17]Loi Taubira.
[18]...été en partie vidée de sa substance... Notamment en ce qui concerne le volet sur *l'indemnisation des États et des descendants d'esclaves"* (pyepimanla.com).

responsibilities. You know, in all this, that we are not alone. We were ready to rally round these provisions, we always are, but it seems that the discussions yesterday showed that this approach was not likely to satisfy those who are negotiating in particular for the Africans...[19] (discours-publics.vie-publique.fr)

Charles Josselin does not exclude the possibility of France participating in reparation for slavery, but he clearly shows the overall position of France, demonstrating its reluctance to assume financial responsibility for her role in the slave trade and colonisation.

The United Kingdom, taking a more radical stance than France and the rest of the European Union, declared through its head of delegation, Valerie Ann Amos,[20] that it was ready to use harsh words to condemn the slave trade which was the pillar of the British Empire, but cannot describe it as a crime against humanity, because that has legal implications. (The Guardian, September 3 2001) Other European countries such as the Netherlands, Spain and Portugal, acting as allies of the United Kingdom, expressed a similar position.

---

[19]*En ce qui concerne la question des excuses...Nous étions prêts à retenir, pour notre part, la formule qui avait été proposée par la présidence belge de l'Union européenne qui était que la conférence de Durban, au nom de tous ceux qui avaient perpétré ces atteintes à la dignité, présente ses excuses. Cette formule avait l'intérêt d'englober, j'allais dire, tous ceux qui ont une part dans ces responsabilités. Vous savez bien que, dans tout cela, si nous avons la nôtre, nous ne sommes pas seuls. Nous étions prêts, si vous voulez, à nous rallier à ces dispositions, nous le sommes toujours, mais, il semble que les discussions hier ont montré que cette formule n'était pas de nature à satisfaire ceux qui négocient, notamment, pour le compte des Africains...*

[20]Baroness Valerie Amos, born in British Guiana (now Guyana) in South America on 13 March 1954, is the 18th and present UN Under-Secretary-General for Humanitarian Affairs and Emergency Relief Coordinator. She was previously British High Commissioner to Australia and Leader of the House of Lords and Lord President of the Council, after being made a Labour life peer in 1997. Following her appointment as Secretary of State for International Development in May 2003, she became the first black woman to sit in the Cabinet of the United Kingdom. When Gordon Brown became Prime Minister in 2007, she was nominated EU special representative to the African Union. She was subsequently appointed Under-Secretary-General for Humanitarian Affairs and Emergency Relief Coordinator.

The United States Secretary of State, Colin Powell,[21] offered support to the French and British positions when in his declaration, he considered it:

...not correct for Africans to demean themselves and those who suffered from both slavery and colonialism by insisting on financial reparations. [...] Africa should be concerned about what it can make of its future, rather than continue to be a prisoner of the past, instinctively attributing its present parlous state to the past as if the continent were helpless. (The Independent, 29 August 2001)

Colin Powell's argument, rejecting Africa's claim for financial compensation might seem surprising as an African-American, unless you consider his position in the United States government at the time of the statement. The nature of American politics and diplomacy, did not allow him, as Secretary of State to campaign for or support reparation openly.

The West thus uniting affirmed their categorical opposition to Africa's claim for financial compensation for their role in slavery and colonialism. In fact, most delegates from the West seemed to be more interested in discussing ways and means of combating the contemporary forms of discrimination, such as those circulating on the Internet or even the "discriminatory" policies of President Robert Mugabe against the white farmers in Zimbabwe.

---

[21]Colin Luther Powell was born in Harlem, a neighbourhood in the New York City borough of Manhattan on April 5, 1937, to Jamaican immigrant parents, who stressed the importance of education and personal achievement. He is an American statesman and a retired four-star general in the United States Army. He became the 65th U.S Secretary of State, and served under President George W. Bush from 2001 to 2005. He was the first African-American to occupy that post. During his military career, Powell was National Security Advisor from 1987 to 1989, Commander of the U.S. Army Forces in 1989 and Chairman of the Joint Chiefs of Staff from 1989 to 1993.He was the first, and so far the only, African-American to serve on the Joint Chiefs of Staff.

The financial aspect of reparation was widely publicised before the Durban conference. In spite of this publicity and the apparent unity of African delegates for financial compensation in their regional preparatory meetings before Durban, discordant voices appeared at the conference. Almost everyone agreed that slavery, colonialism and apartheid be qualified and recognised as "crimes against humanity" and that reparation be taken into account, but their opinions differed on the nature of the reparation to be undertaken. Two main groups emerged: the one which campaigned vigorously for financial compensation and the other which advocated the total cancellation of the external debt of African countries, increasing development aid and an apology. Zimbabwe, Namibia, Zambia, the non-governmental organisations on the continent and the African Diaspora from the United States and the Caribbean took firm positions in support of financial reparation, while Senegal, Nigeria and South Africa appeared more moderate, in favour of cooperation and assistance. The South African delegation favoured this latter group, perhaps for the sake of diplomacy, because it was the host country. South Africa occupied, at the same time, a particular position, being victim of all the three issues in question, namely the slave trade, colonisation and apartheid, even if reparation proper to apartheid was being taken care of by the South African government's Truth and Reconciliation Commission (TRC). It encouraged Africans to take a common position so that reparation took the form of at least aid for economic development. South Africa's position was expressed by the then Deputy President, Jacob Zuma, (now President since 2009) that the nature of the compensation should be determined by the commitment of the perpetrators of the three crimes to contribute to economic recovery by financing and aiding development projects in Africa, particularly the New Partnership for Africa's Development (NEPAD) project.

Yet, before Durban Africa had taken a firm common position vis-à-vis reparation during regional meetings, as when the Heads of State and Government of Member States of the African Union met on the issue of reparation in Dakar, Senegal in 1992 and 2001, and in Abuja, Nigeria, in 1993, when the Abuja Proclamation was made. In Geneva too, during the second and third sessions of preparatory committee meetings for Durban in May and June 2001, African representatives collectively opted for financial compensation.

Contrary to all that, some African leaders expressed a different. For example, Nigerian President Olusegun Obasanjo expressed the opinion at the Durban conference that financial compensation was not a rational option in the event that the perpetrators would offer excuses. (panafricanperspective.com). The Senegalese President, Abdoulaye Wade also held a completely different position from those of most African delegates. He recognised that "... a great injustice had been done to Africa; slavery and colonisation impoverished the continent, which largely explains our delay, to the point of plunging our continent into another calamity: debt, probably as tragic as slavery."[22] (panapress.com). Despite this recognition, Wade did not want to entertain financial compensation; he further declared:

I am opposed to any claim for monetary compensation. The wrongs done to black people cannot be measured in billions of dollars ... I will not associate myself with any request for money; that is accounting on paper. We cannot evaluate these wrongs in monetary terms. That is insulting...the effects of slavery continue to be to the detriment of the continent.[23] (ibid)

---

[22] ...qu'une grande injustice a été faite à l'Afrique, que l'esclavage et la colonisation ont appauvri, ce qui explique largement notre retard, au point de plonger maintenant notre continent dans une autre calamité, la dette, probablement aussi tragique que l'esclavage.
[23] Je suis opposé à toute demande de réparation pécuniaire. Les torts faits au peuple noir ne

Wade, who enjoyed the attention and support of the Western media during the conference, remained adamant in his position. He considered the repentance of Europe enough and qualified as "absurd" any claim for financial compensation, especially for slavery, because such a crime cannot be measured in monetary terms and hence could not be compensated by money. Wade confirmed that Africans also practiced slavery and racism, a proposition which considerably weakened the continent's claim for financial compensation.

Anglo-Saxon newspapers capitalised on that point straight away. Michael Gove, a reporter from the The Times, ironically recalled that Ivorians ransacked shops belonging to Senegalese in Abidjan, damages for which Côte d'Ivoire has still not paid compensation. (The Times, 3 September 2001). The Daily Telegraph also published an editorial on September 3, 2001, in which the author, Barbara Amiel, argued that the only purpose of the conference was to extract money from the rich countries to fill the pockets of "despots" in the Third World. In the United States, the Wall Street Journal on 5 September 2001, argued that Sub-Saharan Africa intended to address the issue of reparation, but the way Uganda, under the administration of Idi Amin Dada, treated Asians, after decolonisation, or the fate today of the white farmers in Zimbabwe, must be remembered.

The series of "Bantu" xenophobic attacks against African immigrants in South Africa in 2008, in which more than 60 people died, mostly foreigners, and the recent attacks that started in Durban in April 2015 in which South Africans looted foreigners' properties and attacked immigrants mainly from other African countries: the Democratic Republic of Congo, Mali, Mozambique, Nigeria, Senegal, Zimbabwe,

peuvent être évalués en milliards de dollars…Je ne m'associerai jamais à une demande d'argent, c'est de la comptabilité sur papier. On ne peut pas en termes monétaires évaluer ces torts. C'est insultant…les effets de l'esclavage continuent de sévir encore au détriment du continent.

Somalia…, killing seven people, would have been used by some critics in the West to discredit Africa's reparation claim.

The opinions of Presidents Obasanjo and Wade neither helped nor pleased financial reparation campaigners from the continent and the Diaspora, simply because it complicated their position. Shehu Sani, a journalist at the Daily Trust and president of the Civil Rights Congress of Nigeria, considered President Obasanjo's proposition "unreasonable and shameful" for the African continent.

Slavery has created more emotions in the African Diaspora than on the continent; the representatives from the Diaspora thus rejected the views of President Wade. Mère Jah, an activist in the Movement for the Return of the Diaspora (MRD),[24] argued that Wade was not mandated by the Diaspora to speak on their behalf. It was above all for the children of deportees to express themselves on the subject. (panapress.com).

Despite contestations and the strong opposition of the West, the report of the conference, acknowledged that:

> … slavery and the slave trade, including the Trans-Atlantic slave trade, were appalling tragedies in the history of humanity not only because of their abhorrent barbarism but also in terms of their magnitude, organised nature and especially their negation of the essence of the victims,…that slavery and the slave trade are a crime against humanity and should always have been so, especially the Trans-Atlantic slave trade and are among the major sources and manifestations of racism, racial discrimination, xenophobia and related intolerance, and that Africans and people of African descent, Asians and people of Asian descent and indigenous peoples were victims of these acts and continue to be victims of their consequences…. (11)

The same recognition was made of colonialism and apartheid, that:

---

[24]*Mouvement de Retour de la Diaspora.*

... colonialism has led to racism, racial discrimination, xenophobia and related intolerance, and that Africans and people of African descent, and people of Asian descent and indigenous peoples were victims of colonialism and continue to be victims of its consequences. ...that apartheid and genocide in terms of international law constitute crimes against humanity and are major sources and manifestations of racism, racial discrimination, xenophobia and related intolerance, and acknowledge the untold evil and suffering caused by these acts and affirm that wherever and whenever they occurred, they must be condemned and their recurrence prevented. (12)

At this point, two important questions arose. First, why did the West refuse to formally apologise, after having recognised that the effects of the slave trade, colonisation and apartheid are among the factors contributing to lasting social and economic problems in Africa? Secondly, why did Africans and the African Diaspora fail, despite their enthusiasm to have the West agree to pay compensation as reparation? To answer the first question, let us acknowledge that Western countries did not want to apologise and individually accept the phenomena as crimes against humanity for fear of being prosecuted. In fact Britain alluded to that fear when its spokesperson at the conference evoked "legal implications." If the West formally apologised as demanded by Africans, that would most probably open the way to court cases seeking financial compensation, which for the Western delegates was to be avoided at all cost. Professor Alioune Tine of the Cheikh Anta Diop University in Dakar, Executive Director of RADDHO[25] and Coordinator of African NGOs, also evoked a similar point that Western delegates were manoeuvring to avoid giving a legal basis to Africa's demand for reparation. On behalf of

---

[25]*Rencontre Africaine pour la Défense des Droits de l'Homme – African Assembly for the Defense of Human Rights.*

African NGOs, he argued that slavery and colonialism should:

...be recognised as a double holocaust and crime against humanity and ...demand compensation from the West for the plunder of raw materials, forced displacement of populations, inhumane treatment and the current poverty in Africa, the fruit of this history of crime and theft.[26] (cran.ch)

As compensation, Professor Tine claimed the cancellation of the debt of African countries and the financing of development projects on the continent. These propositions, which echoed Chief Moshoud Abiola's view, were supported by the members of the Africa Group who believe that the former colonisers must assume their moral, economic, political and legal responsibilities, by participating in African reparation (ibid).

However, the Western countries' refusal to formally apologise did not prevent African-Americans from filing court cases against the United States government and some private companies involved in the slave trade. Even the declaration of the Durban Conference recognising slavery, colonialism and apartheid as crimes against humanity, was a potential source of legal engagement and might generate legal proceedings.

The answer to the second question is not very obvious, but we can assume that Africa has been so affected by its historical relation with the outside world, especially the West, vis-à-vis the slave trade, colonialism and apartheid that its capacity to act independently and constructively has been drastically weakened, to the point of being damaged, especially in the political or economic domains. Because of poverty, precariousness, general economic problems of the

---

[26] ... *soient reconnus comme un double Holocauste et crimes contre l'humanité et ...exigeons réparation de la part de l'Occident pour le pillage des matières premières, le déplacement forcé des populations, les traitements inhumains et la pauvreté actuelle de l'Afrique, fruit de cette histoire de crimes et de spoliation.*

continent engendered by these phenomena and the unfavorable, imbalanced and indoctrinating nature of Africa's relationship with the West, it is always difficult for Africans to collectively and effectively advance the interests of the continent, especially when dealing with the West, which has dominated it so much especially in the political and economic domains for centuries.

In the final declaration, delegates at Durban agreed to include terms that merely expressed apology and deep regret for the immense human suffering and the tragic plight of millions of men, women and children because of slavery, colonialism, apartheid and genocide. (Report 23). Therefore it did not explicitly call for apology from the nations that benefited from the slave trade and colonialism, thus unambiguously rejecting reparation.

The controversy of Africa's reparation claim

In discussing reparation for slavery of Sub-Saharan Africans, there is this tendency to concentrate on the Trans-Atlantic slave trade, and to neglect the existence of the Trans-Saharan slave trade. It is clear that the Western countries were not the only ones to reduce black people to slavery; the Arabs did it too for centuries. It is therefore reasonable to argue that if the West was solely responsible for the colonisation of Africa, it should not be the only one held responsible for enslaving Sub-Saharan Africans. Professor Wole Soyinka pointed out the paradox created by the implication of North Africa in slavery, on Africa's claim for reparation, in his work, *The Burden of Memory and the Muse of Forgiveness*:

Sitting on the commission as a member of the International Committee on reparations was a Tunisian diplomat, an Arab, and he found himself compelled to confront the paradox of his presence as a member of that committee. His response was a safe one, not original but safe....He simply countered with the proposition that, since we are all victims of colonial oppression, we should act together in solidarity against the common oppressor, and obliterate that part of our divisive history. (46)

Therefore, if there is to be any form of reparation for slavery of black people, all those who committed the crime should be legitimately concerned. The Arab world should not be exempted, because they were deeply involved in it as well. Also, as President Wade fittingly pointed out in Durban, although unfavourably to Africa's claim, slavery still existed in Sub-Saharan Africa. This in reality has the consequence of encouraging Western delegates not to feel guilty or obliged, inferring that the West had no moral lessons to learn from a continent which continued to reduce its own people to slavery. The French chief delegate at Durban, Charles Josselin, alluded to this point in his remarks when he stated, "You know, in all this, if we have ours, we are not alone." [27]

Who would compensate the slaves in Sudan, Mauritania and even the women and children employed in Côte d'Ivoire and Benin, for being reduced to slavery and forced labour? This question was humiliating for a people struggling to get compensation on the grounds that their ancestors were enslaved.

Another discomforting truth for Africa is that while African slaves were captured by Europeans and Americans, they were occasionally captured in collaboration with Africans. If black people were bought by whites, they were sold by African leaders too. This collaboration or complicity existed; yet Africans who participated in the slave trade against their own people did not benefit from it from a progressive point of view, because, in working with the Europeans to capture and sell their fellow citizens, they were depriving themselves, unconsciously of course, of their own indispensable factors of production and reproduction, just to acquire textiles, mirrors and weapons, which only encouraged them to wage war on their neighbours in order to capture more slaves, instead of engaging themselves in the business of production, commerce and trade.

Some have also been wondering whether financial compensation should be made to the present generation of Africans who are not direct victims of slavery and colonialism, and how it should be made. To whom exactly should compensation for slavery be paid? How should the exact number of victims be determined? How would the injury be evaluated? Questioned about these, an African diplomat in Brussels responded: ... "We Africans can't start to push them saying we need this money; we can't quantify it..." (Personal interview, 20 June 2007). However he continued to express the view that:

---

[27] "*Vous savez bien que, dans tout cela, si nous avons la nôtre, nous ne sommes pas seuls.*" See page 40

If the Catholic Church can pay millions of dollars on behalf of priests who abused children, well I don't see any reason why there should be no compensation for taking out the best brains from Africa, the most able-bodied people, forced them to work in plantations, that are still benefiting, especially the Americans. And who toiled in Europe, forced them to fight in world wars. (ibid)

Beyond these statements, the identification of beneficiaries, especially with regard to slavery, preoccupied the diplomat. This appeared problematic, because of the diversity and dispersion of victims. African-Americans are claiming reparation from the United States government. What should be done about the other victims living in the Caribbean? Another difficulty to overcome is the fact that the perpetrators of this crime are not alive. Is it fair that the current generation pay for the evil perpetrated by its ancestors, while the acts in question were then not "illegal"? Michael Givens, son of a former Confederate veteran of the American Civil War, admitted that his ancestors actually owned slaves, but he would not apologise for them, since their practice was legal at the time they were doing it. (The Guardian, 3 September 2001) On the occasion of the bicentenary celebrations of the abolition of slavery in March 2006, British Prime Minister Tony Blair made a similar statement that: "It is hard to believe what would now be a crime against humanity was legal at the time" (Daily Mail, 26 November 2006).

These arguments might be interesting; however they are not reasonably justifiable from a moral point of view, not even from a logical one. There was no universal declaration of human rights at the time of the slave trade, but universal natural morality and logic are not at all compatible with such treatment. The Declaration of Independence of the United States, written by Thomas Jefferson in June 1776, stated in its introduction: "… We hold these truths to be self-evident, that all men are created equal, that they are endowed by their

51

creator with certain unalienable rights, that among these rights are Life, Liberty, and the pursuit of happiness..." (archives.gov) Yet this was the very time when France, Britain and the 13 English colonies in North America, and many other Western countries were engaged in the slave trade, reducing their fellow humans of a different race to slavery. It was even the moment that the Trans-Atlantic slave trade reached its peak. In addition, Jefferson, the author of the Declaration of Independence, and George Washington, who was commander of the American militia, among others, held several blacks in perpetual bondage. The West was therefore aware of the obviousness of natural morality and logic, that all human beings are created equal and that their Creator granted them all, without exception, the right to be free and to pursue happiness. The fact that the United States and some other Western countries, notably Britain, France and Portugal reduced black people to slavery, while very much aware of this natural endowment of all with life, liberty and the pursuit of happiness, can be described as outright hypocrisy and/or racism.

Slavery gave birth to colonialism and harsh and restrictive laws which were extremely racist in their nature, such as the *Code Noir*[28] in France, the Black Code[29] and the "Jim Crow laws"[30] in the Southern United States, and apartheid in

---

[28]The *Code Noir* passed by King Louis XIV of France in 1685, which defined the conditions of slavery in French colonies, also restricting the activities of free Negroes.

[29]Black Codes were restrictive laws passed by Southern States in 1865 and 1866, after the Civil War, with the aim of restricting the freedom of African-Americans, and of compelling them to work in a labour economy based on low wages

[30]The Jim Crow laws were racial segregation laws enacted in by Southern states and municipalities, between 1876 and 1965, that legalized segregation between blacks and whites. The Supreme Court ruling in 1896 in *Plessy* v. *Ferguson* that separate facilities for whites and blacks were constitutional encouraged the passage of discriminatory laws. Under Jim Crow laws, therefore, African-Americans were relegated to the status of second class citizens. Railways, public waiting rooms, restaurants, theatres, public parks... were segregated; separate

South Africa, against black people. It stood out as the most severe form of racism that generated tremendous socioeconomic problems, therefore requiring reparation for the devastations it caused. The issue of reparation for the slave trade must not disappear with the death of its perpetrators. The fact that the properties acquired by the slave traders were transmitted to their descendants, and the dispossession just like the wealth was equally transferable and indeed transferred to the descendants of the slaves, as President Mbeki put it in his opening speech at the Durban World Conference against Racism, there should be compensation to the descendants subjected to the injustices. Compensation to the victims of slavery, colonialism and apartheid, phenomena that the international community, including the descendants of the perpetrators themselves, described as crime against humanity, should not be pending indefinitely.

For crimes committed a very long time ago, the descendants of the perpetrators would most probably feel less compelled to agree to pay reparations, as we have noticed in the arguments, especially when it comes to financial compensation and when these crimes or injustices had been legally accepted by the societies at the time they were committed. However, reparation for slavery and colonialism should, as we have indicated, not solely be concerned with punishing the perpetrators as a way of correcting the injustices; it should also be geared towards remedying the contemporary consequences of the injustices or crimes. Therefore, it must also identify the effects and consequences of these injustices for reparation to be remedial and meaningful.

Financial or material reparation would always encounter complications and contestations, which might render them difficult to realise, as was the case in Durban. As we have

---

schools, hospitals, and other public institutions, generally of inferior quality, were designated for blacks. Jim Crow was not a person; it was named after a popular 19th-century minstrel song that stereotyped African-Americans

seen, reconciliation was a prerequisite, yet Africa still has to reconcile with the West on these historical facts, because their relationship is not based on sincerity and social justice. If this reconciliation fails, the reparation that Africans on the continent and the Diaspora are claiming will be difficult to obtain, if not impossible. Another difficulty that emerged was the global nature of the demand for reparation, especially concerning slavery, constituting the biggest difference between the demand for reparation for slavery and other forms of reparation already made. As reconciliation is a precondition, the more reparation is forced on the parties concerned, the more its realisation will be liable to problems. It is very difficult to give money and also more difficult to formally apologise, especially if the apology has legal implications.

Concerning these complications, some commentators argued that it was too late to seek reparation, especially for slavery, which was abolished more than 200 years ago, at least in Britain. However, colonialism only ended approximately 60 years ago, and considering the case of the Jews, compensation to the victims of the Holocaust was not made by Adolf Hitler, under whose administration the crime was committed, but by those who came after him, i.e. by the Germany of Konrad Hermann Joseph Adenauer, as Randall Robinson argues here:

> For twelve years Nazi Germany inflicted horrors upon European Jews. And Germany paid. It paid Jews individually. It paid the state of Israel. For two and a half centuries, Europe and America inflicted unimaginable horrors upon Africa and its people. Europe not only paid nothing to Africa in compensation, but followed the slave trade with the remapping of Africa for further European economic exploitation. European governments have yet even to accede to Africa's request for the return of Africa's art treasures looted along with its natural resources during the century-long colonial era. (Robinson 204)

Compensation for slavery and colonialism can therefore be done in a similar manner to other forms of reparation, such as that made by Germany to the Jews and the acceptance by Congress to pay reparation to century-old American-Indian claims.

The points of view of President Obasanjo and Wade at the Durban Conference were thus controversial, because a cheque repaired, at least partially, the crime of the Holocaust perpetrated against the Jewish people during World War II. Colin Powell's notion of Africans being "prisoners of the past" was also more political than rational. Therefore, despite all these difficulties, the evidence of the debt is there. Africa's claim for compensation for slavery and colonialism is justified. It is just the ways and means of the reparation that have to be agreed on.

We have indicated that despite the numerous complications caused by circumstances and international relations, Africa's claim for reparation was reasonable. Countries and companies which practiced and benefited from the slave trade and colonialism, should contribute both materially and morally to alleviating their consequences on the people of African descent.

The Declaration and Programme of Action of the Durban Conference against Racism identified the slave trade, colonialism and apartheid as the major sources and manifestations of racism and racial discrimination, as well as the causes of poverty, socio-economic inequalities and marginalisation of which Africans and people of African descent have been victims. After having condemned slavery, colonialism and apartheid, the conference expressed profound regret for the suffering and evils inflicted on the people of African descent by the institutions of slavery, colonialism, and apartheid. The conference further indicated that some States had taken the initiative to apologise and to pay "reparation, where appropriate, for grave and massive violations committed" (Report 23). Also as a means of healing these "dark chapters in history and facilitating reconciliation," the international community was invited "to honour the memory of the victims of these tragedies." However, only a few countries took the initiative to express remorse or present apologies, consequently the recommendations "call on all those who have not yet contributed to restoring the dignity of the victims to find appropriate ways to do so." (Report 24) The final statement did however not specify the names of countries which apologised or promised to pay reparation. The United Kingdom was, however, certainly not part of these countries given the behaviour of its delegation at the conference.

The conference recognised a moral obligation relating to the historical responsibility of these acts, but only vaguely demanded the States concerned to take appropriate measures to end the lasting consequences of the practices in question. What is the impact of these statements and recommendations on Africa's quest for reparation in general?

This is the first time the international community formally recognised the slave trade, colonialism and apartheid as crimes against humanity and as tragedies in the history of mankind. Some African observers believe that the conference and its declaration are a positive step towards African reparation. According to a Kenyan delegate, Amina Mohamed, Head of Mediation with the West at the conference, "Africa had a rendezvous with history. We have an agreement on a document that is far from satisfactory, is terribly imperfect, but that provides a basis to build on, and I think, for the first time, the dignity of the black man has been recognised" (carolcooper.org).

Professor Alioune Tine also welcomed the declarations of the conference as "great victory for Africans and African-Americans, even if the final declaration does not contain the formal "apology" by former colonial powers."[31] (rfi.fr)

However, the declaration and programme of action, as we have seen, led to no concrete proposal. They only vaguely recommended and invited the participants to take the initiative and express remorse or apology and recognise the need for assistance for Africa's development programmes.

It was clear at the end of the conference that financial reparation, which was the gist of Africa's claim and the source of much controversy in Durban, no longer seemed to be a possibility in the immediate future. The behaviour of

---

[31] C'est une grande victoire pour les Africains et les Africains-Américains, même si la déclaration finale ne présente pas les "excuses" formelles des anciennes puissances coloniales.

the Western delegation at Durban showed that they were reluctant to engage in financial or material compensation. And the more time passed, the more its possibility diminished. Some Africans even emphasised the difficulty of determining the nature of reparation. Interrogated about the kind of reparation desirable for Africa, an African diplomat in Brussels expressed the view that. ... "it's the Europeans themselves who should come up with an idea of what they should do to compensate for what their forefathers did" (Personal interview, 20 June 2007).

The diplomat did not clarify the nature or form that financial reparations should take. He continued, however, to reject the activities of the World Bank and the IMF, and advocated a sort of "Marshall Plan" for Africa. He argued that when the loans accorded to African countries by these inter-governmental financial institutions expire or the money finishes, they:

...have to come back for another loan. This is why so many countries in Africa have debt. Because this initial loan has not been sustainable. They have to be coming for more loans. That was not the idea of the Marshal Plan in Europe. The Marshal Plan in Europe put up infrastructures. They put up things in place to develop industries, to develop the people in the area, to have employment for a long-term. That was what the Marshal Plan was about and that was why Europe stood after the Second World War. That's the same thing we are asking for now, it's as simple as that, trade liberalisation, you know. The Structural Adjustment programme has to have a development oriented agenda. Develop infrastructure, develop capacity, create jobs, enhance small and medium enterprises, develop manufacturing industries, people would not be dependent on you. But most of these Europeans (laugh), I mean, want us to be dependant, because if we are not dependant on them half of them lose their jobs as consultants. (ibid)

Therefore, if the authors of the crimes are unwilling to engage in financial compensation, before being coerced by law to do so, their historical and moral responsibility, and the universal principles of humanity and morality require today that at least they act and show solidarity vis-à-vis the countries that have suffered the injustices in question. It is the problems of poverty, under-development, marginalisation in international relations, and economic disparities that are in question here. Thus, the recommendations of the conference identified projects to contribute to development in the societies that were affected.

We have said that financial reparation would be difficult, even impossible to acquire without the willingness of both parties to reconcile. Thus, the relationship between the two parties through the establishment of effective dialogue in an atmosphere of mutual respect and sincerity to clarify and facilitate the process is very important.

However, five years after this conference, some Western politicians have still been reluctant to formally apologise. Britain refused to apologise for its role in slavery, in spite of the appeal of the Archbishop of York to formally do so. During the ceremony of the bicentenary of the abolition of the Slave Trade Act (1807),[32] Tony Blair declared: "Personally I believe the bicentenary offers us a chance not just to say how profoundly shameful the slave trade was - how we condemn its existence utterly and praise those who fought for its abolition - but also to express our deep sorrow..." (Telegraph, 29 November 2006).

However, the former Mayor of London, Ken Livingstone on 24 August 2007 publicly apologised for London's role in the slave trade declaring: "You can look across there to see the institutions that still have the benefit of the wealth they created from slavery" (dailymail.co.uk). Pointing towards the

---

[32]A bill abolishing the slave trade and prohibiting the introduction of new slaves in all British possessions

financial district of London, Mayor Livingstone broke down in tears, and claimed that London was still tainted by the horrors of slavery.

The British Prime Minister, just a year after creating the Commission for Africa, which we considered as a serious and genuine device for African reparation, merely expressed "deep sorrow" for the role played by the United Kingdom in the slave trade, simply qualifying it "profoundly shameful." When Chancellor Gordon Brown started his campaign to get to 10 Downing Street, he declared: "…the days of Britain having to apologise for its colonial history are over."(opendemocracy.net) Four months before that, at the British Museum, Gordon Brown declared that the UK "should be proud of the Empire" (Daily Mail, London, 14 September 2004).

In a tweet on Wednesday, 7 May 2014, the Vice President of UMP[33] in France, Thierry Mariani, suggested that "the abduction of the young Nigerian girls by the Islamist sect Boko Haram,[34] which threatens to sell them as 'slaves' shall exonerate the West for slavery."[35] Mariani went on further to say […] "My reaction on Twitter is simply a reminder of a

---

[33]*Union pour un Mouvement Populaire* (The Union for a Popular Movement) is one of the two major contemporary political parties in France, majorly competing with the centre-left Socialist Party. UMP is centre-right and was formed in 2002 as a merger of several centre-right parties under President Jacques Chirac. Nicolas Sarkozy who led the party won the 2007 presidential election but was defeated by François Hollande's Socialist party in the 2012 presidential elections.

[34]A militant organisation founded by Mohammed Yusuf in 2002, based in the north-east of Nigeria, north of Cameroon and Niger, known by its Hausa name Boko Haram, which means 'Western education is forbidden'. Its Arabic name is "People Committed to the Propagation of the Prophet's Teachings and Jihad" - (Jama"atu Ahlis Sunna Lidda'awati Wal-Jihad) in Arabic. Boko launched military operations in 2009 to overthrow the Nigerian government and establish a "pure" Islamic state governed by sharia to stop Westernisation. Its founding leader was killed in police custody the same year. He was succeeded by Abubakar Shekau.

[35]*L'enlèvement de jeunes Nigérianes par la secte islamiste Boko Haram, qui menace de les vendre comme « esclaves », doit déculpabiliser l'Occident quant à l'esclavage.*

61

historical truth. Indeed, slavery in Africa is a practice that dates back well before the arrival of the West."[36] (lemonde.fr)

In a joint statement, two Socialist Party deputies Yann Galut and Alexis Bachelay judged Thierry Mariani's attitude immoral for an elected Republican, and asked that he be removed from his position as Vice President of the UMP. They argued that:

These statements fall in line with the strategy of the National Front, whose mayor has banned Villers-Cotterets participating in Remembrance Day of slavery, claiming a ritual of guilt. If slavery already existed in ancient societies, and if human trafficking remains a critical problem today, denying the importance of industrial slavery organised by Europeans in the modern era and during part of the nineteenth century is highly problematic.[37] (ibid)

By these statements, it was clear that the West, especially Britain and some statesmen in France did not abandon their firm position on the issue of reparations that their delegates defended in Durban in 2001. It seemed thus easier for Tony Blair and the United Kingdom to establish a Commission for Africa than to simply formally apologise for Britain's role in the slave trade and colonialism.

Aidan McQuade, director of Anti-Slavery International, demanded that the history of the slave trade be taught in schools, arguing that:

They could also make measures of reparation towards the communities and countries which have been impoverished and

---

[36]*Ma réaction sur Twitter est simplement le rappel d'une vérité historique. En effet, l'esclavage en Afrique est une pratique qui remonte bien avant l'arrivée des Occidentaux.*

[37]*Ces déclarations s'inscrivent dans la droite ligne de la stratégie du Front National dont un maire a refusé à Villers-Cotterets de participer à la journée de commémoration de l'esclavage, prétextant un rituel de culpabilisation. Si l'esclavage existait déjà dans les sociétés antiques, et si la traite des humains reste aujourd'hui un problème crucial, nier l'importance de la traite industrielle organisée par les Européens à l'époque moderne et pendant une partie du XIXe siècle est hautement problématique.*

devastated by the Trans-Atlantic slave trade, and they could have much more concrete measures in terms of eradicating contemporary forms of slavery in the world today. (Daily Mail, London, 29 November 2006)

Sub-Saharan Africa could have relied on the influence of several African countries, including Nigeria and South Africa on the international stage to vigorously advance its claim for reparation. However, President Olusegun Obasanjo and Vice-President Jacob Zuma, we have seen, felt that financial compensation was not a rational option, because it risked dividing Africans on the continent and those in the Diaspora. President Wade of Senegal also categorically dismissed the idea of financial compensation for the slave trade calling it "absurd," because such a crime perpetrated cannot be compensated in monetary terms. In this perspective, Africans should resort to other forms of reparations.

We have said that the purpose of reparations for slavery, and colonialism should not solely be based on acquiring money from the West and Arabs for the crimes they committed against Africans, but also to correct the negative effects of these contemporary historical crimes. It should also be geared towards addressing the current problems they engendered. The cancellation of Africa's public debt should therefore be a determined factor of African reparation, because it would also help alleviate Africa's poverty, promote its effective integration into the global economy, solve the problem of technology transfer from the West, and promote industrial development and investment in social infrastructure. The moral aspect of reparation which we have identified incorporates apology, remorse, excuses etc.

France has already taken a step towards moral reparation when it decided to commemorate slavery on May 10 of each year, starting from 2006. The UK, however, is not yet ready to commemorate the victims of slavery and colonialism, but has initiated a commission to help Africa in its process of reparation, even if that is not oriented directly to slavery and colonialism. Africa, as the major beneficiary, should also ensure the determination of the international community to redress the problems caused by the phenomena in question. To advance the process of post-colonial reconciliation and reparation, Africa must establish a new vision of its relations with the West, based on realism. Therefore, the financial component that preoccupied the continent more at the Durban conference should not be a mathematical factor of reparation. There is also a socio-political aspect of African reparation which relates to African people regulating their own conduct by adopting self-discipline, the respect of the rules and regulations that govern them and applying rigour and professionalism in their activities and development projects. African attitude and approaches should not only be based on the Western notion of diplomacy and politics, purely foreign to African values; in other words, African principles and methods should be appropriately linked to the socio-cultural values of the people, even if other required values could be strategically incorporated in the context of globalisation. Many Africans believe that reparation also entails the West refraining from supporting dictatorial regimes, even if these regimes disregard human rights and democracy; as long as these governments submit to the vested interests and desires of the West, the lives and wellbeing of Africans do not count. Africans must therefore equally adhere to appropriate democratic values and resist all forms of interference in the internal politics of their countries by foreign parties. Because some believe that Africans are themselves responsible for allowing foreign governments to interfere in African internal politics:

They are more culpable than anyone else. Since the dawn of independence, they failed in confronting the West, because those who would not give in were either killed, overthrown, removed through polls manipulated by the West's unjustified sanctions. So that is why most of them fear to confront the

West, forgetting that somebody has to sacrifice for the betterment of the future. (Interview, 15 July 2007)

Reparation, as we have claimed, should not be left solely in the hands of the political elite; the civil society should also participate in it under democratic values, as exemplified by the strategies of the Economic Community of West African States (ECOWAS).[38]

The relationship between Africa and its former colonisers, which operates through organisations such as the Commonwealth and the *Organisation Internationale de la Francophonie* was considered another type of reparation, because it provided aid and assistance to African countries in the form of solidarity and cooperation. However, these associations have equally been accused of exercising cultural domination of Africans through their cooperation and assistance, because the socio-economic benefits enjoyed by African countries through their membership of these associations are considered to be comparatively less important than the submission and loss of Africa's socio-economic values. Indeed, some observers believe that associations like the Commonwealth and the *Francophonie* play a "minimal" role in African development ... "Very little. They are involved only in so-called governance projects and a little in education. We need infrastructural developments to enable governance to prosper" (ibid).

Now more than 13 years after the Durban Conference against Racism, Africa's demand for compensation as reparation for slavery, colonialism and apartheid seems to

---

[38]The current ECOWAS vision 2020 project, which is a long-term strategic plan seeking to provide a reference point for an integrated development approach for the West Africa region in line with a bottom up strategy of involving community citizens for a people-centred Community development approach, is a demonstration of more commitments by the West African people to closer integration. For example through the West African Civil Society Forum (WASCOF) and other similar civil society groups, the ECOWAS Commission is promoting the active involvement of ordinary citizens in the affairs of their Community.

have fallen into oblivion. At Durban II, held in Geneva in 2009 as a follow-up to Durban 1 (World Conference against Racism, Racial Discrimination, Xenophobia and Related Intolerance), the issue of reparation for slavery, colonialism and apartheid was over-shadowed by the pretext that the conference would promote an anti-Semitic agenda. For example, the USA, Canada and Italy all boycotted Durban II, and all the Western delegations, except Norway, walked out during the Iranian President Mahmoud Ahmadinejad's speech against Israel. Most observers consider this charge of anti-Semitism as an excuse to avoid Durban II and hence the question of the debt owed by the West and the Arabs to Africa. This is ironically using the Holocaust, which was an enormous racist atrocity, to sabotage other racist atrocities, but of greater magnitude combined, i.e. the slave trade, colonialism and apartheid.

The Durban and Geneva texts were in fact unbinding and hence had no strength and the Durban Declaration, we have seen, explicitly stated that the countries concerned are not under any legal obligation, but a moral one to take appropriate measures to end the damaging effects of colonialism and slavery.

However the British government, in June 2013, was forced to recognise that Kenyans were tortured by British colonial rulers during the Mau Mau uprising, resulting in the killing of thousands in the 1950s, and it pronounced its regrets; consequently, the victims would be paid £20m as compensation (bbc.com).

To convince the West to assume its responsibility, Africans, for their part, must first assume their own responsibility and raise their conscience and awareness, to strengthen their capacity for good governance and the promotion of democracy, because bad governance and dictatorship destroy the people, and then kill the nation. Africa must also overcome the problem of modern slavery in countries like Sudan, Mauritania and even Mali, as well as child trafficking, even if child trafficking might not strictly be considered as slavery in the real sense.

The overall goal of reparation being to correct the inequalities, and economic and social marginalisation of the African continent caused by the phenomena in question, African decision and policy-makers should collaborate with the entire world, especially leaders of the West to address these problems, basically through African initiatives. The resources of the countries should effectively be invested in priority domains such as health, education, infrastructural development...

Conclusion

The African Diaspora claimed reparation for slavery before continental Africa, so far in vain, but the struggle continues with the existence of organisations like N'COBRA and related reparation movements, as well as the advocacy of numerous personalities such as Rev. Jesse Jackson, Min. Louis Farakhan, Randall Robinson...

In the early 1990s, the Organisation of African Unity, through the initiative of Chief Moshood Abiola of Nigeria, formally defended the thesis for reparation that the 1993 Abuja conference proclaimed afterwards. The Abuja Proclamation as the original source of Africa's claim for reparation was made at a time when the continent was still a victim of increasing marginalisation in the economic and political spheres. Africa's demand for reparation was centered on the slave trade and colonialism, but we have seen that reparation goes beyond the mere issues of slavery, colonialism and apartheid, to take into account contemporary issues such as the public debt incurred by the continent, international relations and trade and sustainable development.

According to the Abuja Declaration, the problem caused by slavery, colonialism and the post-colonial relations between Africa and the West "...is not a thing of the past, but is painfully manifest in the damaged lives of contemporary Africans from Harlem to Harare, in the damaged economies of the black world from Guinea to Guyana, from Somalia to Surinam." (panafricanperspective.com) It goes further to show that the West has a moral debt towards the African continent, requiring reparation in the form of investment, the cancellation of Africa's public debt and contribution to Africa's overall development programme. In this perspective, the question of compensation should take into account the redressing of the negative effects of slavery and colonialism on the people of African descent.

In the absence of the United States,[39] the Durban conference recognised slavery, colonialism and apartheid as "crimes against humanity," as well as sources of inequality, poverty and racism. The West admitted its historical role vis-à-vis the slave trade, colonialism and apartheid, and deplored the socio-economic consequences of this role on the people of African descent. However, most countries involved in the slave trade and colonialism, including the United Kingdom and France, refused to formally apologise and certainly did not want to commit themselves to any form of financial compensation. The United States government, even before quitting in protest against the draft resolution comparing Zionism to racism, threatened to withdraw if a mandate for reparation was applied. At Durban, the West therefore simply acknowledged that the socio-economic problems in Africa emanated from their relations with the continent, which entailed the slave trade, colonialism and apartheid, but did not genuinely consider participating in redressing these problems. Moreover, since this international conference, nothing concrete has been done about Africa's claim for reparation, because its final Declaration did not call outright for reparation and an explicit apology from the nations that benefited from the slave trade and colonialism.

The conference, under the direction of the United Nations, was intended to be "action oriented," and the majority of delegates from Africa and the Diaspora were determined to have their voices heard in trying to have the wrongs of the past corrected. However, it was very difficult for them to even get a formal apology from the West, because Africa's claim for financial compensation was

---

[39]The delegations of the United States and Israel left the conference because of the draft resolution comparing Zionism to racism, as in the 3379 UN resolution on the Elimination of All Forms of Racial Discrimination, which determined Zionism as a form of racism and racial discrimination.

complicated by too many controversies, generated by the lack of reasoning and sheer reluctance of Western decision-makers on the one hand, and the lack of vision and unity on the issue amongst Africans on the other. The aspirations for the conference eluded those committed to its success; thus the people of African descent have wondered why the West should reject the idea of compensating them, when the Jews, as Randall Robinson and other advocates highlighted, were paid for the genocide they suffered at the hands of Nazi Germany principally. The meeting lost momentum as a result of the inability to reach consensus on a multitude of issues, especially questions regarding reparations for slavery; the proposed Zionism equals Racism equation concerning Palestine and Israel, and the marching out of the United States delegation as a manifestation of their historic and uncompromising support of Israel also weighed heavily on the result of the conference. The attack on the Twin Towers of the World Trade Center in New York and the Pentagon in Washington, D.C. on September 11, 2001 just a week after the conference ended completely overshadowed the significance of the event.

Africans having centred their claim for financial compensation solely on the West, tending to exonerate the Arabs, which renders the reparation claim precarious and fragile. To genuinely and impartially claim reparation, it has to be levied on all the parties who perpetrated the crimes. The dispersed nature of the potential beneficiaries has also complicated Africa's demand for reparation. As we have noticed the most controversial issues which almost derailed the event, were reparation for the Trans-Atlantic slave trade and the Zionism equals Racism issue on Israel and Palestine. African countries, just like Europeans, were largely divided over the substance and procedure of reparation. Zimbabwe headed a campaign by a few African countries and some African-American organisations and individuals against Western countries that were extensively involved in the slave trade, to demand reparation for slavery in the form of an apology and cash payments. The South African government and some other countries on the African continent preferred reparation in the form of developmental assistance. The attitudes of individual African leaders such as Presidents Abdoulaye Wade and Olusegun Obasanjo, who qualified financial compensation as an irrational option because it risked dividing Africans and the Diaspora, played a central role in the controversies. Moreover, President Wade's view that Africans have themselves practiced slavery and are still enslaving their fellows, complicated the claim for reparation, especially financial compensation. Before all the complications are resolved, Africa's claim for reparation risks remaining a long unresolved issue.

This is substantiated by the fact that more than thirteen years after the Durban Conference, nothing tangible has come out of the demand for compensation. At the second Durban Conference reparation for slavery and colonialism was trivialised and overshadowed by the issue of anti-Semitism. However, the history of the relationship between Africa and the international community, especially the West, legitimised reparation, at least in the form of cancellation of Africa's public debt, which is an essential step towards reducing its socio-economic problems.

It would be absurd to deny the fact that the slave trade and colonialism in Africa were brutally inhumane treatments. The discrimination and racism they engendered have been devastatingly humiliating for the African peoples. The debts incurred, and the degradation that these exploitations generated, whose nature and causes have been very clear, are fundamental sources of under-development, poverty and marginalisation of the African peoples.

The trend that reparation should take might be difficult to be agreed on and accepted by all the parties concerned, but it is legitimate and essential for Africa and its Diaspora to end the marginalisation and precariousness of which they have been victims for centuries. The identification of beneficiaries and payers should not be a complication because governments and some private companies that were involved in the slave trade and/or colonisation are identified. The West has been reluctant to directly participate in reparation, but it should not totally evade its responsibility, and the Arabs should be on board. They should collaborate with Africa as a moral gesture to help redress the continent's socio-economic problems. If we take the North American Marshall Plan in Europe after World War II as an example, Europe was not colonised by the United States. It could even be considered the other way round, since it was Great Britain that had established thirteen colonies in North America. The Marshall Plan, however, helped to reconstruct Europe's ruins from World War II. Western governments are both legally and morally responsible for what their ancestors committed in Africa, simply because the wealth created by the slave masters and colonialists during the slave trade and colonial exploitation has been transferred from generation to generation, and the wealth has been protected by successive governments in the respective countries, hence the involvement of both the State and individual families.

The Commission for Africa initiated by Prime Minister Tony Blair might be considered as a good mechanism of reparation for Africa, but it did not have the same conviction as the Marshall Plan, due to the delicate nature of international politics and trade, as well as the relative inability of Britain to shoulder the programme alone. The report's appropriate calling for a fresh shape of partnership between the West and Africa "based on mutual respect and solidarity," can be qualified as one of the most serious reviews of Western policy in Africa. It accurately evoked the undemocratic nature of the functioning of inter-governmental institutions like the WTO, the IMF and the World Bank, suggesting that these institutions give more voices and accord greater representation on their Boards of

Administrators or Governors, and to make strategic leadership and decision-making the responsibility of the political leadership of their Member States. The recommendations of the reports, amongst others, on trade liberalisation, corruption and aid had long been called for by Africans, but had never been considered by Western countries. The recommendations of the Commission, especially concerning subsidies on agricultural products, met strong opposition from the G8 members and even British businesses that were worried about more regulation. Also the Treasury of the United States opposed the commission's recommendation for 100% debt cancellation. The United States equally rejected the Commission for Africa's calls for an immediate end to EU/USA subsidies on local products, especially on cotton and related agricultural products. Also, some G8 countries such as France, Germany and Italy benefitted enormously from the Common Agricultural Policy of the European Union, which was considered by the Commission for Africa's reports as one of the most protectionist trade regimes in the world. These complications hampered the efforts of Prime Minister Blair's Commission as part of the effective apparatuses of African reparation.

Reparation at international level can take the form of debt cancellation, evoked by the United Nations to facilitate Africa's integration in the international economy on good terms. Countries that are most in need of this option should be identified by the African Union in collaboration with the international community. The G8 established a list of 18 countries, of which 14 are in Sub-Saharan Africa.[40]

Reparation is not charity; the international community, notably the West and the Arab World, who so exploited Africa in terms of slavery and colonisation, owe the continent compensation to repair the damages they caused,

[40] Mali, Mauritania, Senegal, Niger, Burkina Faso, Ghana, Benin, Ethiopia, Uganda, Rwanda, Tanzania, Madagascar, Mozambique and Zambia.

which would help Africa to participate effectively in global socio-political and economic activities. Thus, the Arab world cannot be exempted from participating in African reparation, due to their role in the Trans-Saharan slave trade. The first step should be the recognition of the historical wrongs committed as moral reparation, and that was superficially done in Durban. The international community should then try to vigorously campaign for the eradication of the stereotypes and stigma pasted on the black man through these phenomena.

Civilization does not only symbolise economic and technological advancement, and Western democratic values, but also social justice and simple and constructive reasoning towards other humans. The international community, especially the West, should play a role in African reparation, by emulating Prime Minister Tony Blair and his Commission for Africa, for the continent to address its marginalisation and other socio-economic problems in spite of Britain's refusal to formally apologise for its role in the slave trade and colonisation. For this to be achieved, the cancellation of Africa's public debt, the promotion of education, health and foreign investment in Africa, especially in infrastructure, the fight against HIV/AIDS, access to markets and transfer of technology as suggested in Durban and then recommended by the Blair Commission for Africa, are essential and should be supported by the West as a form of reparation.

Reparation will not only liberate Africa and its Diaspora, it will also emancipate the conscience of the communities which participated in the slave trade and colonialism. In monetary terms, without an effort to end racism and racial discrimination, as well as the modern factors that have exacerbated the marginalisation of Africa, it would not be sustainable. All the countries that participated in slavery and colonialism should perpetually commemorate the memories linked to these phenomena by incorporating programmes and lessons of history in schools, to remind citizens of these wrongs and their effects on both communities. It is a responsibility and duty to recall to memory, honour and morally repair.

We have said that Africa's claim for compensation is justified and obvious, for the simple reason that African people were deprived of their values and their material and social resources. In a moral perspective, it is vital that the truth be established for Africa and mankind at large, because African history vis-à-vis slavery, colonialism and apartheid is a lesson for all, a truth that should be shared by all, for all to assume their responsibilities and roles. During the Durban conference, the West recognised these phenomena as "crimes against humanity," but refused to apologise and agree to pay financial compensation. This refusal by the authors of slavery and colonialism to participate in repairing the damages caused by these phenomena in Africa, symbolised the fourth phase of African dispossession, because as Frantz Fanon stated in his work *The Wretched of the Earth,* the raw materials that were used in Europe's development were mainly from the colonies; therefore:

Europe is literally the creation of the Third World. And when we hear a European Head of State declare hand on heart that he must help poor underdeveloped peoples, we do not shake with recognition. On the contrary we say to ourselves: It is a fair compensation that will be paid to us. Also we do not accept that aid to underdeveloped countries is a 'Sisters of Charity' programme. This assistance must be an acceptance of two things - awareness by those colonised that it is owed to them, and by the capitalist powers that indeed they should pay. That if, by choice–not to mention ingratitude - the capitalist countries refused to pay, then the implacable dialectic of their own system would threaten to suffocate them.[41] (72, 73)

---

[41]*L'Europe est littéralement la création du tiers-monde. Et quand nous entendons un chef d'État européen déclarer la main sur le cœur qu'il lui faut venir en aide aux malheureux peuples sous-développés, nous ne tremblons pas de reconnaissance. Bien au contraire nous nous disons : C'est une juste réparation qui va nous être faite. Aussi nous n'acceptons pas que l'aide aux pays sous-développés soit un programme de 'sœur de charité'. Cette aide doit être la*

Also recalling Nelson Mandela's words in 2005, alluding to African reparation, "Overcoming poverty is not a gesture of charity. It is an act of justice."

African reparation requires the removal of the scars of centuries of oppression, exploitation and marginalisation of people of African descent. It therefore entails developing a mechanism to strengthen and support the functioning of existing Pan-African institutions through the African Union, to nourish the African Renaissance and promote progressive regional integration to give the continent more autonomy and independence. African reparation is therefore an obligation for Africans first, as descendants of the victims of the phenomena in question. It is a way of expressing the African personality and incorporating it into the overall system of politics and commerce. Africa must initiate the process of reparation for the West to follow. Therefore, if the West has a responsibility towards redressing Africa's socio-economic problems and marginalisation, Africa has a greater responsibility towards its own reparation. In that case, whether the West and the Arab world agree to contribute to African reparation or not, it lies plainly in the hands of Africans themselves, and entails strengthening the African Renaissance. African reparation should not be limited to the economic sector, since development also encompasses political and cultural aspects. It should promote African cultures and the democratisation of government by improving the electoral system, giving the appropriate freedom to the people and the media, and accelerating the fight against corruption, which is a global phenomenon, and therefore not exclusive to Africa.

Slavery dehumanised Africans, while colonialism and apartheid exploited and deprived them of their resources

consécration d'une double prise de conscience, prise de conscience par les colonisés que cela leur est dû et par les puissances capitalistes qu'effectivement elles doivent payer. Que si, par intelligence – ne parlons pas d'ingratitude – les pays capitalistes refusaient de payer, alors la dialectique implacable de leur propre système se chargerait de les asphyxier.

before upsetting their overall development. The trauma generated by these phenomena has handicapped Africa, leading to its people's lack of confidence in themselves and feeling of abandonment. But Africans must free themselves and not stand indolently waiting for the West or Arabs to take them out of their marginalisation, precariousness and poverty. Africa must struggle on its own without helplessly depending on others, because as we have highlighted, African reparation is an African continental responsibility before being the responsibility of the Arab world and the West. Therefore, Africans should be more pragmatic to become genuine nationalists, and cease being simple nationalist figures.

African reparation also requires engaging African citizens to understand the politics and policies that govern them. Africans in the process should work according to their cultural values and the transformative aspects of these values. The individual African should be part of the collective Africa. The indispensable factors of African reparation in the larger context of socio-economic development are self-discipline, self-respect, respect of democratic values and the rule of law, rigour, professionalism and genuine adherence to African socio-cultural values.

Bibliography

Primary sources

Personal interview. 20 June 2007.

Personal interview. 15 July 2007.

A/RES/52/111 Resolution adopted by the General Assembly on Third Decade to Combat Racism and Racial Discrimination and the convening of a world conference against racism, racial discrimination, xenophobia and related intolerance. Washington DC, 18 February 1998

A/CONF.189/12 Report of the World Conference against Racism, Racial Discrimination, Xenophobia and Related Intolerance. Durban, 31 August - 8 September 2001.

Secondary sources

Books
A.

Ajayi, J F Ade. *General History of Africa Volume 6*, Paris: UNESCO, 1989.

Ashcroft, Bill, Gareth Griffiths, and Helen Tiffin, ed. *Post-Colonial Studies Reader.*London: Routledge, 1995.

F.

Fanon Frantz. *Les damnés de la terre*, Paris: Éditions la Découverte, 1968.

Ferro, Marc ed. *Le livre noire du colonialisme XVIe – XXIe siècle : de l'extermination à la repentance*, Paris : éditions Robert Laffont, 2003.

Finley, Moses I. *Ancient Slavery & Modern Ideology*. Princeton: Markus Wiener Publishing Inc, 1998.

K.

King Martin Luther Jr. *Why We Can't Wait*. United Kingdom: Penguin, 1991.

L.

Lovejoy, Paul E. *The ideology of slavery in Africa*. Beverly Hills, California, London: Macmillan, 1981.

Lovejoy, Paul E. *Transformation in slavery: a history of slavery in Africa, 2nd ed.* Cambridge: Cambridge University Press, 2000.

M.

Mazrui, Ali A. *The Africans: A Triple Heritage*. Boston: Little Brown & Co. 1986.

N.

Ngugi wa Thiong'o. *Decolonising the Mind: The Politics of Language in African Literature.* London: J. Currey; Portsmouth, N.H.: Heinemann, 1986.

Ngugi wa Thiong'o. *Moving the Centre: The Struggle for Cultural Freedoms.* London: J. Currey; Portsmouth, N.H.: Heinemann, 1993.

R.

Reader, John. *Africa: A Biography of the Continent.* London: Hamish Hamilton, 1997, 840p.

Rodney, Walter. *How Europe Underdeveloped Africa.* Washington D.C.: Howard University Press, 1982.

S.

Soyinka, Wole. *The Burden of Memory, the Muse of Forgiveness.* Oxford: Oxford University Press, 2000.

Periodicals

Deroche, Sylvie. "Esclavage. Réparations controversées." *L'Intelligent* n°2097, (20-26 mars 2001) : 15-16.

Ghechoua, Afafe. "Esclavage pour ou contre les réparations?" *L'Intelligent* No 2122, 11-17 sep. 2001 : 4.

Web pages

Comité pour l'Annulation de la Dette du Tiers Monde. *Juillet*, 2007 <http://www.cadtm.org/img/pdf/vademecum2005b-2.pdf>

European Network on Debt and Development (Eurodad). "Détails machiavéliques : les implications de la proposition du G7 sur la dette. Briefing d'Eurodad aux ONG, Bruxelles." 14 June, 2005. 30 Aug. 2013. <http://www.eurodad.org/uploadstore/cms/docs/G7_accord_FR.pdf>.

Carrefour de Reflexion et d'action d'Action Contre le Racisme Anti-Noir (CRAN). "Le CRAN s'insurge contre la "haine de l'Occident" attribuée aux Africains et dénonce le Prix littéraire des droits de l'Homme décerné à l'ouvrage!" <http://www.cran.ch/04_PageCentrale/2_Communiques/2008/Communique CRAN_JeanZiegler_25Dec2008.pdf>.

Online Newspapers

Arnot, Chris. "David Richardson: Chained to the past: The bicentenary of the abolition of the slave trade does not mean it is over." *The Guardian,* Jan. 9, 2007. 20 Aug. 2007.

<http://education.guardian.co.uk/academicexperts/story/0198553 8,00.html>

Atlantic Blackstar. "Barbados Takes Lead in Fight For Reparations for Slavery in the Caribbean." *Atlantic Blackstar*, 6 Nov. 2012. 6 Aug. 2013.
<http://atlantablackstar.com/2012/11/06/barbados-takes-lead-in-fight-for-reparations-for-slavery-in-the-caribbean/>.

BBC News. "Guyana Calls for reparations." *BBC News*, 27 Mar. 2007. 14 Feb. 2013.
<http://www.bbc.co.uk/caribbean/newq/story/2007/03/070327 _jagdeore parations.shtml>.

Best, Tony. "The Case for Reparations." *Carib News*, 6 Mar. 2013. 12 Feb. 2014.
http://www.nycaribnews.com/news.php?viewStory=3672>.

Bowcott, Owen. "Africans call for slavery reparations." *Guardian unlimited*, 20 July 2002. 10 Aug. 2007
<http://www.guardian.co.uk/unracism/>.

Brogan, Benedict. "It's time to celebrate the Empire, says Brown." *Daily Mail*, 15 Jan. 2005. 20 Dec. 2011.
<http://www.dailymail.co.uk/news/article-334208/Its-time-celebrate-Empire-says-Brown.html>.

Cessou, Sabine. "Durban : compromis final." *RFI*, 10 Nov. 2001. 20 Dec. 2012.
<http://www.rfi.fr/actufr/articles/021/article_12534.asp>.

Cox, James. "Aetna, CSX, FleetBoston face slave reparations suit." *USA Today*, March 25 2002. 10 Feb. 2014.
<http://usatoday30.usatoday.com/money/general/2002/03/25/slav e-reparations.htm>

Daily Mail. "Government pays $1billion compensation to Indian tribes over century-old claims to money and land." *Daily Mail*, 12 Apr. 2012. 12 Dec. 2013.
<http://www.dailymail.co.uk/news/article-2129056/Government-pays-1billion-compensation-Indian-tribes-century-old-claims-money-land.html>

Daily Mail. "Livingstone breaks down in tears at slave trade memorial." *Daily Mail*, 24 Aug. 2007. 4 May 2014.
<www.dailymail.co.uk/news/article-477337/Livingstone-breaks-tears-slave-trade-memorial.html>.

David Smith. "Blair: Britain's 'sorrow' for shame of slave trade." *The Observer*, 26 November 2006. 14 May 2014.

<http://www.theguardian.com/politics/2006/nov/26/race.immigr
ationpolicy>
Jamaica Observer. "UWI principal wants CARICOM to seek
reparation for slavery." *Jamaica Observer*, 12 February 2013. 12 Dec.
2013.
<http://www.jamaicaobserver.com/latestnews/UWI-principal-
wants-CARICOM-to-seek-reparation-for-
slavery#ixzz2Mqi9W08m>.
Molotsky, Irvin. "Senate Votes to Compensate Japanese-American
Internees." *New York Times,* April 21, 1988. 11 Apr. 2014.
<http://www.nytimes.com/1988/04/21/us/senate-votes-to-
compensate-japanese-american-internees.html.>
Le Monde, "Mariani se sert du rapt au Nigeria pour "déculpabiliser"
l'Occident sur l'esclavage." *Le Monde,* May 07 2014. 15 May 2014.
<http://www.lemonde.fr/politique/article/2014/05/07/thierry-
mariani-entend-deculpabiliser-l-occident-quant-a-l-
esclavage_4412853_823448.html>
McGreal, Chris. "Britain blocks EU apology for slave trade" *The
Guardian UK,* 3 Sept. 2001. 10 Nov. 2013.
<http://www.guardian.co.uk/world/2001/sep/03/race.uk>.
Nessman, Ravi. "World Conference Against Racism 2001: Deal
Reached." *The Associated Press,* 09 Aug. 2001.
<http://carolcooper.org/racism.php>.
Nyatsumba, Kaizer. "Like spoilt brats they threw tantrums and
threatened to boycott the racism conference." *The
Independent/UK.*Aug 29, 2001. 15 Dec. 2012.
<http://www.commondreams.org/views01/0829-05.htm>.
Panapress. "Protestation contre les propos du Pr Wade sur la
réparation." *Panapress.* 24 Aug. 2010. 10 Dec. 2010.
<http://www.panapress.com/Protestation-contre-les-propos-du-
Pr-Wade-sur-la-reparation--13-615182-17-lang4-index.html>.
Panapress. "Wade réaffirme son opposition à toute forme de
réparation pécuniaire." *Panapress,* 12 August 2001. 10 Dec. 2012.
<http://www.panapress.com/Wade-reaffirme-son-opposition-a-
toute-   forme-de-reparation-pecuniaire--13-614534-17-lang4-
index.html>.
Petre, Jonathan. "Blair's deep sorrow for slavery is not enough."
Telegraph 29 Nov. 2006. 28 Aug. 2007.
<http://www.telegraph.co.uk/news/main.jhtml?xml=/news/2006
/1/28/nslave28.xml>
Robinson, Mary. "Africa Needs Fair Trade, Not Charity" *YaleGlobal
online,* 23 Aug. 2005.10 Feb. 2007.

<http://yaleglobal.yale.edu/display.article?id=6210>.
UN, "Reparations should be made for African slave trade, Antigua and Barbuda tells UN." *UN News Centre*, 24 Sep. 2011. 15 Oct. 2013. <http://www.un.org/apps/news/story.asp?NewsID=39770&Cr= slave&Cr1=#.VTPhKXk8bIV>.
Woollacott, Martin. "The time for apologies and restitution is not yet over." *Guardian unlimited*, 22 Aug. 2002. 4 Mar. 2007. <http://www.guardian.co.uk/unracism/>.
Wintour, Patrick. "Blair fights shy of full apology for slave trade." *The Guardian*, Nov 27, 2006. 31 Aug. 2007. <http://www.guardian.co.uk/guardianpolitics/story/01957709,00.ht ml>.

Online books.
Ajayi, J.F. Ade. *Unfinished Business: Confronting the legacies of Slavery and Colonialism in Africa*. The South-South Exchange Programme for Research on the History of Development (SEPHIS), Centre for Studies in Social Sciences, Calcutta (CSSSC). Amsterdam/India: 2002. 22 Aug. 2007. <http://www.cssscal.org/Publications.html>

Online articles.
Brendon Piers, "A moral audit of the British empire." *Open Democracy*, 6 Nov. 2007. 22 Nov. 2014. <https://www.opendemocracy.net/article/globalisation/visions_reflections/british_empire>
Conyers, John Jr. "Statements from April 6, 2005 briefing: The Impact of Slavery on African Americans Today." *The U.S. House of Representatives*, 6 Apr. 2005. 20 Aug. 2007. <http://www.house.gov/conyers/news_reparations.htm>
Commission for Africa. Our Common Interest, *Commission for Africa*, March 11, 2005. 15 Dec.2014. <http://www.commissionforafrica.info/2005-report>
Commission for Africa. "Still our Common Interest." *Commission for Africa*, September 12, 2010. 10 Aug. 2014. <http://www.commissionforafrica.info/articles/still-our-common-interest-the-commission-for-africa-launches-new-report>
Encyclopedia Britannica "Talion". 15 Feb. 2012. <http://www.britannica.com/EBchecked/topic/581485/talion>
Farrakhan, Louis. "A case for reparations: Add it UP!" <http://www.finalcall.com/columns/mlf/reparations.htm>

Gifford, Lord Anthony. "The legal basis of the claim for Reparations, A paper Presented to the First Pan-African Congress on Reparations." Abuja, Federal Republic of Nigeria, 27-29 Apr. 1993. 10 Feb. 2007 <http://www.arm.arc.co.uk/legalBasis.html>.

Greenhill, Romilly, Watt, Patrick. "Real Aid: an agenda for making aid work." Action Aid (UK). 09 Jun., 2005. 05 Dec. 2012 <www.actionaidusa.org/Action Aid Real Aid.pdf.>

"Issues: Reparations. bill H.R. 40, Commission to Study Reparation." <http://conyers.house.gov/index.cfm/reparations>

Mark Weber. "West Germany's Holocaust Payoff, to Israel and World Jewry." *Institute for Historical Review.* <http://www.ihr.org/jhr/v08/v08p243_Weber.html>

National Coalition of Blacks for Reparations in America (N'COBRA). "The Abuja Proclamation." *N'COBRA*, Apr. 27-29, 1993. 20 Dec. 2012 <http://www.ncobra.org/resources/pdf/TheAbujaProclamation.pdf>

"The Declaration of Independence."<archives.gov/national-archives- experience/charters/declaration.html>.

N'COBRA. "The National Coalition of Blacks for Reparations in America." <http://katrinareader.org/national-coalition-blacks-reparations-america-ncobra>

N'COBRA. "The Abuja Proclamation." <http://www.ncobra.org/resources/pdf/TheAbujaProclamation.pdf >